Everest England

Published by AA Publishing, a trading name of
AA Media Limited, Fanum House, Basing View,
Basingstoke, Hampshire, RG21 4EA, UK.

First published in 2019

A CIP catalogue record for this book is available from
the British Library.

ISBN: 978-0-7495-7923-4

Publisher: Phil Carroll
Editor: Donna Wood
Art Director: James Tims
Designer: Tracey Freestone
Reprographics: Ian Little
Illustrations: Sarah Farooqi

Printed and bound in the UK by Clays

A05575

theAA.com

EVEREST
— E N G L A N D —
29,000 FEET IN 12 DAYS

PETER
OWEN JONES

For Martin Thomas
A man of love

Contents

The Climbs

▲1 St Enodoc's Church and Brea Hill, Cornwall: 203 feet

▲2a Bronn Wennili (Hill of Swallows), Bodmin Moor, Cornwall: 1,321 feet

▲2b Yes Tor and High Willhays, Dartmoor, Devon: 1,263 feet

▲3 Great Hangman and Holdstone Down, Devon: 2,172 feet

▲4a Glastonbury Tor, Somerset: 394 feet

▲4b Cheddar Gorge to Beacon Batch, Somerset: 2,461 feet

▲5a Crickley Hill, Gloucestershire: 787 feet

▲5b Cleeve Hill, Gloucestershire: 935 feet

▲6 The Malvern Ridge, West Midlands: 3,313 feet

▲7a Caer Caradoc, Shropshire: 961 feet

▲7b Pole Bank, Shropshire: 1,754 feet

▲8 Kinder Scout, Peak District, Derbyshire: 2,051 feet

▲9 Haworth to Hebden Bridge, West Yorkshire: 1,142 feet

▲10a Hebden Bridge to Stoodley Pike, West Yorkshire: 965 feet

▲10b The Calf via Cautley Spout, Cumbria: 2,018 feet

▲11a The Cheviot, Northumberland: 2,093 feet

▲11b Dungeon Ghyll to Pavey Ark, Cumbria: 2,008 feet

▲12 Scafell Pike, Cumbria: 3,221 feet

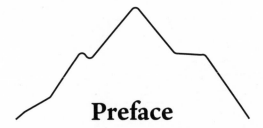

Preface

If you are going to climb around 29,000 feet to the summit of Everest then there are a few things that will need attending to before you go. I don't wish to be prescriptive but, in case it's of use, what follows is an account of how I – just about – didn't come unstuck on my journey.

I think it is important to do the climbs all in one go and not have a rest day. I made the ascent in 12 days but there is no reason why it shouldn't take more or less time. And as each day passes the journey deepens, physically and mentally.

I travelled by car between the mountains and hills. Next time I would like to travel using public transport.

As with any physical challenge, it is imperative to have the right kit. The most important item is,

of course, a good pair of boots that have already been worn in. These boots will also need to be waterproofed. It is always wise to pack a spare pair of laces, too.

I walked carrying a day-pack in which there was a waterproof top and waterproof trousers as well as a whistle and a torch. I ate food I had prepared and brought with me on the hills every day and carried enough water for one day, which for me is one litre.

I did take a mobile phone, but it was for emergency use only and I kept it switched off for the entire journey. I did not use it as a navigational aid. For all navigating I used OS maps. Taking the right maps with you each day is extremely important. There are illustrative maps in this book to give an impression of the more difficult routes but these should never be used for navigation.

All the routes are pretty much on public paths but it is important to know that we share this land with nesting birds, with marbled white butterflies, with foxes and stoats, and they have just as much right to be here as we do. Leave the flowers to make their seeds.

I booked all the accommodation beforehand. That means that in some instances the accommodation for the night was sorted out that morning. I stayed in the cheapest places I could find. I did not stay with friends as I wanted as much time alone as possible.

This journey does come with very real risks. Human beings die on mountains and hills, especially in bad weather. It would be prudent therefore to call in each evening, especially if you are walking alone.

For me this was just as much a spiritual journey as a physical one. And while I did not set off with an intention, a journey like this will bring to the surface much of what has not been attended to. This is just as much about beauty as it is about pain.

I decided before setting off that I would not watch, read or listen to the news, listen to the radio or look at any form of weather forecast. I did listen to music while journeying between the hills, and you will find a piece of music for each day at the start of each chapter. All these pieces of music are extremely meaningful to me, and they contributed to the journey.

The evenings I spent alone, as quietly as possible. I lay down at nine every night. I did not drink alcohol or smoke hash.

The book is laid out in 12 day sections. Each day contains descriptions of what I saw, felt and imagined while I walked and climbed, followed by more practical directions for those who wish to walk the same paths. The ascent figure given for each of the climbs is accumulative, taking you closer and closer to the desired height.

I chose to walk the height of Mount Everest because on this planet it is as high as our feet can take us.

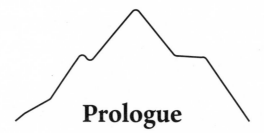

Prologue

There is no way of knowing when it might happen, but in most human lives it happens at least once – an event or a chain of events leads us out beyond the fences we have wired, apparently for our own protection, and takes us above base camp.

Usually it is the brutality and injustice of love and death that shake us out of our normal life and its constructed or inherited order. 'Normal', you see, is just an agreement that serves a solid purpose – to keep us safe and apparently on track.

But when we have been wounded to the point where we are doing little more than functioning and surviving, there comes a point where something in us needs to die, although we can carry on like this for years. And should we take this path we become increasingly ghostly. We end up as a stranger to ourselves and the experience of pain, of loss, of betrayal does not cause us to grow – instead we shrink.

Then it is time to leave, *now* it is time to leave, when we are making excuses to remain alone this evening, when the routine that holds the frame of our life comes to define it. This is where the mountains come in, where wilderness, wildness and the storm offer their hand.

Only some of the unknown lies outside of us. Most of the unknown is, in fact, within us, and we have so little time. If we are lucky and stay healthy and love – yes, loving is the healthiest thing we can do – then you and I might live until we are 80 or so, but the truth is, not even our next breath is guaranteed.

In this country around four million people walk every weekend, slightly less in the winter and slightly more in the summer. An average walk lasts between one and three hours. A 12-day walk is something else and a pilgrimage is another thing altogether. In both of them, perhaps, we walk into a different state of being ourselves.

Sometimes a man rises from the supper table
and goes outside. And he keeps on going
because somewhere to the east there's a church.
His children bless his name as if he were dead.

Another man stays at home until he dies.
Stays with plates and glasses.
So then it is his children who go out
into the world seeking the church he forgot.

Rilke

I know people who have taken years to leave and others who have woken up that morning, packed and left within 15 minutes.

The grass is a different colour every day. Depending on rain and sunlight and, of course, the time of year, each blade is green and fierce, this food for horses and sheep.

Beyond the window isn't a floral garden; it is mostly grassed, and then a big hedge at the back separates the fields from the garden. In the hedge next to a tumbledown shed in the corner, just beyond some old apple trees, is half a gate. The hedge on either side has grown round it and through it and it isn't steady, but I am just tall enough to haul myself over, and on the other side I am beyond the garden. I grew up on the plain.

It was a halfway land then, half wild, half farmed. The fields must have been small. In the first one, at the back, is a marshy pond, completely untidy. It is shallow and in the summer the cattle that periodically broke into the garden could almost walk into it. They would stand there seething with flies, among the rushes. As the autumn rains arrived the marsh ran bleak. One heron would occasionally come and stand; a statue from another world. And there were snipe, small and swerving. I never saw them in the sunlight.

The next field holds a big pond. It is surrounded by woods and home to reed and marsh warblers, and whitethroats. There is a path which runs right the way round. The boys from the estate don't tend to come here much any more.

Once, in a blackbird's nest snug and sewn into some gorse leaning over the water was a completely blue egg, and towards the end of that summer one dead swallow washed up on the shore, sodden with water. In the spring great puddles of frogspawn would sit in the shallows, in the reeds out of reach of the fish. They were all eaten. All that remained were two pike. They both died pretty much at the same time, one half swallowed in the other's mouth.

More than anything, the pond is a land of birds. There is constant song. The only time this wanes is perhaps for two weeks in the summer when the air is filled with hundreds of dragonflies who emerge from the pond having transformed from fish into birds. They are mostly brown hawkers but in among them are the vivid blue and green emperors.

In the 16 years of my boyhood I never saw the farmer once, not even a footprint. It was as if the land looked after itself; the cattle came and went, as did great numbers of butterflies. Meadow browns, gatekeepers, holly and common blues, small coppers, small tortoiseshells, painted ladies, small and green-veined whites. It was alive land.

I am probably around six when I make it to the next field. It is a quieter field, the land is more even and there are fewer thistles and barely a butterfly. It also has a pond. This one is surrounded and shaded by hawthorn and blackthorn trees and is home to a pair of moorhens: black-feathered and gangly, feet too big for their bodies. The water here is solemn, it is grey: this is where the foxes bury their kills. In this place there is only one day of summer. Again, I never saw the farmer, fences would appear from time to time around the pond but there were never any tracks.

In the top corner of the field is the edge of a copse and within the copse is another pond. This one has notices around it; the fishing belonged to the Edenbridge Angling Society and occasionally there would be one or two men in heavy clothes sitting alone on the bank next to a rod reaching over the water. They never spoke, never said hello.

I must have been around seven or eight when I ventured into the next field. One autumn it was flush with field mushrooms, and elderly women and men came from the estate and picked basketfuls. This was Melanie's field really. She lived in the big house that sat in the valley underneath it. She was shallow-rooted, she didn't eat all her sweets at once, her house on the plain was separate from other houses. It stood on its own, it was as if every room was on a different level. The doorways had steps in them.

The Kent and Sussex brook was at the bottom of the next field. Ragged and barely flowing, hiding under grass and bramble. This was the boundary – I didn't cross it until I was about 12 years old. On the other side of the brook I left the land of my childhood behind.

The epicentre was the second field. It was as if all life sprung from the pond and it is easy to understand how our fathers and mothers believed just that: believed that the sky spoke and the wind sung songs. I know it was brutal: they all died young until the first seed was intentionally planted; until farming began. We didn't ever leave the forest; we cut it down, we made fields.

But maybe we left something behind. We seem to have inherited a sorrowing, a bereaving. We were wild for far longer than we have ever been tame. We seem increasingly out of place, outcast, walled up in cities barricaded from the consequences of our own behaviour. For the guilty, making peace is a last resort because it calls for accountability. We have yet to make peace with the butterflies, the rooks, the curlew, and the fox, for sure.

Somehow the second field had been left, had not been what is now described as being 'improved'. It had not been rendered mute and there was within it all life, of course, and I was not treated as separate.

And here was the voice of the rain speaking on the surface of the pond. Flowing streams of individual tadpoles moving as one entity, following a path through the water. Yes, and the dancing frenzies of the first spring flies, this is sexual energy. All this reflection, all this being.

In India the holy men and women, the sadhus, gather every 12 years at the Kumbh Mela. Each sadhu belongs to *akhada*, essentially a tribe, and within that tribe there are separate groupings, different gurus. They each have their own encampments but the site never really sleeps on the main festival days when there are upwards of 20 million people present. Every sadhu encampment has a fire and that fire does not go out, it is considered sacred. There are rules about what goes into it and what goes over it. Really it is a memory of when possessing fire was critical, in the time perhaps before human beings had discovered how to create it.

The sadhus are very much the wild beings of the woods. They are the wild men and women – undomesticated, wanderers – and we look over our shoulders at them and know that a few of them speak from the wilderness, speak from the wild places, and are not and have not been completely tainted and compromised by comfort, by life insurance, by sugar.

My friend Andreas Kornevall, founder of the Earth Restoration Service, said to me, 'No one is at the boundaries of civilisation any more. We are all within its folds.' This is an increasingly dangerous place to be, because there is no one speaking from beyond the folds, from beyond the streets and fields. We have lost sight of ourselves, there has been no one calling progress to account.

This is the job of the mystic, the wild man, the women on the hill. They can speak of truth and healing because they see the whole picture, because they are not part of the current conspiracy – whatever that may be. They can speak of the carnage of love, of self-obsession, the killing of butterflies, of the excuses fermented by fear, of cowardice in the face of beauty, and yes, they can and will unmask the gangsters and the narcissists.

The feeling, the thought, is that I need to leave that which I have around me. That which I have constructed is actually the problem, or at the very least reflects the problem. This feeling is not uncommon; it is, however, largely unspoken. While we might know it in a growing sense of unease, it is a desire either for change or for resolution.

It is also an admission that something needs to unravel, in order to be found, and this is where the journey starts. It starts inside. We have to leave.

A little planning is perhaps a luxury. There were three things I consciously left behind on this journey. They were the news, the phone and the weather forecast, so that what was given was what I would be grateful for.

My only rules were that I would say hello to everyone I passed on foot and go to bed at nine.

There are three parts to this leaving: the severance, the challenge and the return.

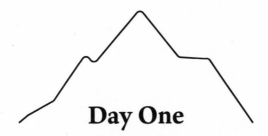

Day One

St Enodoc's Church and Brea Hill, Cornwall (Sea Level)

*Music: 'Could It Be Forever'
by David Cassidy*

At around 15,000 feet, at the base camp of Everest before you climb, it isn't so much of a prayer that is muttered or spoken, it is a bargain that's made.

The Buddhist lama creates an altar, and on it are placed offerings of butter, Marmite, beer and raksi, as well as your boots, your crampons and your ice axe. He burns some juniper.

You pay your respects to the gods of the mountain and, in return, you hope that respect is reciprocated, that your life, your breath, will be protected. It is a plea for mercy. This plea only unfolds within us, can only be uttered, when we we find ourselves in the space between life and death, or when we love completely – when there is nothing else of us that remains hidden or when we are an inch away from death.

It is not a long way back into the time when men and women made offerings to the rivers, to the forest, and bargained with the sea as they still do in Benin before they leave the harbour in Cotonou to fish. It was hard to know what to say, kneeling in the empty church, here at the beginning when everything in preparation is done, when the maps are in folders and the path through the days to come has apparently been decided.

Two hundred years ago, St Enodoc's church was almost immersed in sand, the pre-Christian gods of the sea in league with the wind slowly burying the sky-god's fortress. The parishioners would break in through the roof and hold one candlelit service a year, whispering their offerings just to keep the church legally open. It is now marooned on a golf course, tight grass greens, men in slacks – the dunes have been mowed, the moles murdered. Ten months ago there was a wedding here and the remains of roses, big blue hats and a lake of eyes were opened once again, waiting, the empty pews ingraining what was known, the silence of the inside rekindling scents and sounds of memory.

The bride sat down on the chancel steps; she had their son at her breast. The groom knelt down before her and here they spoke their vows. 'To have and to hold from this day forward, to love and to cherish.' And after all the precision, the art direction, the rehearsing, the choreography about where exactly they were to stand and look into each other and make their promises, this was the way it happened, this was the path it took. It could not have been written, it could not have been planned; it was simply and beautifully how it unfolded.

Everest England

And I have the mountains named and the hills marked in ink, and over and over it I have been, measuring the feet and nursing the metres, and yet all along really I knew it was folly, a piece of paper to hang onto, an order to fall in line behind. So now like a fool and a coward I offered it up, these few drops of ink, this miserly certainty.

What use is protection? Protection from what – from tiredness, from loneliness, from an accident, from my heart giving out, from fear, from the torments of love? From sorrow and the dark, descending stairway? These are all teachings – should they really be avoided, watered down and rendered easy?

The plan said start tomorrow and it's true that if the foundations are messed about with, then the bricks won't fit. From that point on, you don't know what the building is going to look like.

The consequences of following the plan suddenly seemed dreary, a route march from here to Cumbria. There was nothing to wait for, not any more, not now, not when the sky from the church porch was running the clouds over Brea

Hill and flashing citrus light all over the water. Yes. Do it now.

Brea Hill is more of a dune than a hill. It feels as if it has been given – left as an offering by the wind. It is perhaps where the land and the wind meet once a year to exchange gifts. The land gives the gift of freedom to the wind and the wind gives the gift of surety to the land. And over time Brea Hill became big enough not to be moved. It became itself, it was given a name. It rises from the seashore halfway up the Camel Estuary and from the top you would have been able to see the Irish rounding the point, coming to steal women and silver.

Brea Hill is a vantage point closer to the sky, to the visible ocean waiting, always waiting, at the mouth of the estuary. It feels apart and separated from everything around it. Perhaps it is this resonance that drew St Enodoc towards it; maybe it was already a shrine, a holy hill, a thin place, and maybe she had been searching for a while and she knew the place when she found it. She arrived in the 6th century at a time when the population of England had declined to around two and half million. It is strange that in what would have been a predominantly empty landscape these Celtic saints wandered in search of isolation.

The car park in Trebetherick seems almost bigger than the beach. The shop and cafe are closed, the windows haven't been cleaned for a while, they are dull with salt and sand has gathered at the doors. In just 12 weeks' time on a bright blue day, children will be running towards a collection of brightly coloured rock-pooling nets and plastic buckets and walking back to the beach with ice cream all over their cheeks.

The gulls have quietened; they tend to become much less raucous in the afternoon. At dusk they turn into ghosts. In the mornings they take to the rooftops and, as they bend their necks backwards, breathe in and open their beaks to the sky, they become cockerels. It's a beautiful noise.

The tide is in, testing the tattered and broken fence guarding the dunes.

I lifted a blue-coloured stone from the sand and placed it in the side pocket of the day-pack. That is where it ended up. Leather boots and sea water is not a good combination – not for the boots, which had been cleaned and proofed: all part of the plan.

The wooden footbridge on the far side of the beach leads over a sultry stream and into a tunnel of a path, opening and splitting through the marram grass at the base of the hill. It's a hike up the side from the sea, good and steep, dented and scarred by human feet. Brea Hill is a kissing hill; there are not many of them in England. Not many close enough to home and far enough from the front door, from the fire on the beach.

And in the summer under a warm August moon you offer your hand to be held, to hold. You are 14 and on holiday. You've spent the last week posturing, feigning disinterest, jumping from the highest dune, pretending to like Billy Joel: that really hurt. Then there was that attempt to push out beyond the far break on your body board, believing that she might be watching at the time.

You don't actually know it yet but you are going nuts, you have bottled out so many times and spent every available break in the routine between the beach and meals in front of the mirror in the bathroom that your father took you aside and interrogated you about your bowel movements, insisting that if you had diarrhoea it was something you needed to be open about so that other people didn't catch it.

It is now the last night and the three families are together for the final barbecue. By now you are feeling pretty hopeless; I mean, you have hardly spoken to her all week. So after surreptitiously necking a couple of stolen cans you manage to come up with, 'I have heard the view from the top of the hill is really lovely when the sun is going down. Shall we go and see what it's like?'

In another desperate act of bravado you run up Brea Hill and by the time she makes it to the top you are still so out of breath that you can barely speak. So you sit on the top and watch as this incredible star changes colour.

This is the first time you have actually been alone together; something has to break. You have been imagining this moment all week, rehearsing it, but this is the reckoning. You will discover on this evening, on this hill, whether you are the safe but steady type; the practical and attentive type; the fickle bastard or, God help you, the incurable romantic.

The getting up and pretending to stretch was a good move, especially as it meant that when you sat down again you sat right next to her and for the first time you could hear another human being breathing.

Your heart is beating hard.

'I really, really like you.'

'I really like you, too.'

And it isn't fast or rushed, it is as if you knew how to do this all along. She puts her arms around you and you place your lips on hers and she places her lips on yours.

Then she says, 'We'd better go back,' and you both return and acted as if nothing had happened.

On the morning after the wedding the congregation set off from Trebetherick, walking through the fields towards Brea Hill. It is very rare now to see large groups of people walking through the land. It's as if they had left church one hundred years ago and were making their way home, some arm in arm, with children dancing at their sides, having been released from an hour of sitting still.

We shambled up the hill and gathered on the brow and sung a shanty in the sunshine, the bride still wearing her wedding dress.

For this love is our love
yours and mine
heave away all together
and food for us all
both bread and wine
whatever the weather.

Now the wind still has winter in it, the clouds have wrapped the sun and the sea is beginning to steady for the evening, it is good to be far from home.

⌒ **203 feet**

Day One

Directions

One mile
Allow half an hour

▷ There is a good car park on Trebetherick beach or you can park in Trebetherick and cut over the fields from the main road running through the village. Whichever way you choose, it is a very roundabout route.

▷ To reach St Enodoc's church, walk back up the single-track road from the beach car park and you will find the footpath on your right as you head up the hill. This footpath essentially leads around the edge of the golf course before cutting across one of the fairways and through a small and stunted copse up to the wall of the church.

▷ To find the main path up onto Brea Hill from the church, retrace your steps and there on your left you will see a bridge that crosses the small stream. From here the path leads out into the marram grass and then up onto the summit of the hill.

Day One

▷ If the stream is low and the tide is out it is possible to reach the hill by simply walking across the beach at low tide.

▷ Don't forget to pick up a small blue stone from the beach and put it into your pack.

Day Two

Bronn Wennili (Hill of Swallows), Bodmin Moor, Cornwall

Music: 'The Journey' by Geoff Robb

As far as translations from Cornish to English go, the highest point on Bodmin Moor is a notable low point. Bronn Wennili translates from the Cornish as the 'hill of swallows'. It is easy to see the phonetic flow from Bronn Wennili to Brown Willy and maybe this is just the way language travels through time, but it feels as if something has been vandalised. It has.

There has been a process of cultural erosion, an undermining of a marriage, an intimacy, between the land and those who have lived within it for generations. What has happened over time to Bronn Wennili also happened to Uluru, renamed Ayers Rock, which now thankfully is to revert back to its original name. Uluru is sacred to the Anangu people and renaming it after an Australian provisional governor removes any sacred associations. The bottom line is that it is theft.

The road from Camelford leading onto the moor is unusual for a road in inland Cornwall in that it is straight. It is a straight drive towards both the oncoming moor and Rough Tor, rising ever closer. Moorland has a completely different colour palette to the lower-lying field systems that invariably surround it. The moorland colours are the natural complexion of much of the western half of this island. In the far west of Cornwall, between St Ives and Sennen, the fields are too small for tractors and there are hills of stones running above the sea.

To the south of Land's End there is a house under some trees in a small hamlet. The paint is peeling from the walls; it doesn't appear to have electricity. It is the home of a single man in his late 70s. The lean of the south coast of Cornwall means the house has slightly more protection from the incoming winter westerlies; there seems to be more soil. And here, in a snuck in the cliffs, the single man is tending a vegetable plot. It is beautiful, just the fact that it is here; one tiny field in a fervour of brambles and bracken.

As the sun lands on Bodmin Moor it renders it almost orange, water in threads and mirrors turning almost white. The conifer plantation next to the car park is barely green and the grass on the verges next to the trees is just about living. Under the canopy is a dark realm, the floor a dungeon of carcasses and occasional skeletons of birds and rabbits; a place of starvation, a place of depression. In here is a seemingly endless night, a complete absence of tenderness. It is a good decision not to take a walking stick from here.

The path from the car park heads downwards and crosses a stream. The ground beyond is wet and giving. It has rained in the night, washing all of yesterday's footprints away. Sometimes it is comforting to see them.

There is a threshold between the fields and the moor. Within the field systems water is channelled, the flow is arranged and organised. On the moor it roams where it will. There is also a complete change of soundscape. Fields, especially the ones contiguous to woodland, can often hold more sound, all the more so if they have some protection from the wind, but they don't offer the depth of silence and the audible reach of wide-open spaces.

Occasionally a meadow pipit flies low over the winter grass, meaning that there is a nest nearby. There is very little that is green here; the spring growth is waiting underground, the land is the colour of lichens.

To make the height, it is necessary to clamber up onto Rough Tor and from there walk down the valley to the base of Bronn Wennili. Now you are truly beyond the road, away from the edge of the moor and here the stones haven't been collected.

From the summit of Bronn Wennili the laying of the straight road in becomes clear. What must have been a china clay quarry is now a lake, and in front of the lake one single brown farmstead stands surrounded by a moat of small fields.

Cornwall hasn't always been a tourist destination. Once it stood on the edge of the world, and very few people would have known about it or seen this farm. Farms are their own kingdoms; they don't have boundaries, they have borders. They pass through the generations like an axe. The handles change; a new head is bought, but it is still the one axe; the haft smoothed in some cases with the sweat of your father's hands, your mother's hands.

Many farming families still live out their entire lives on the one farm. They grow up there, they grow old there. Each farm is an island, it has its own scent. It is set apart, often with no visible neighbours. You can shout as loud as you like and turn the music up – life runs on the rhythm of sowing and growing.

You live with dogs and mud, milk and seeds, and the carpet under the table was put there by your grandmother, and the shelves in the bathroom were made by your grandfather. And they made love, they made *you* in the room you now sleep in, warm in her arms, waking to offspring songs from the sons of the warblers that sang to greet an older dawn.

Everything is held in this space, everything comes to pass. You have ingested how the sun moves across the kitchen walls on an afternoon in September and can read how the colours born on Bronn Wennili announce the coming of rain, the death of lambs and arriving heat. There is no other home.

On a clear day from the top of Bronn Wennili the north and south coasts of Cornwall are clearly visible but the distance is smeared with a heavy Atlantic air and the sea has disappeared.

There are increasingly fewer and fewer petrol stations away from the main routes. A young man with a red beard holds a bucket in one hand and a sponge in the other; he is cleaning one of the two petrol pumps standing under the sky on the A395.

He looks as if he hasn't slept, or the two chocolate bars and the packet of prawn cocktail-flavoured crisps he called breakfast are running his system down. He is out of place here, he is lost, and both of these states are exceptionally good teachers. The rites of passage that are meant to open the door from the boy to the man, the girl to the woman, are as faded now as the wisdom that recognised their value. Boys, especially, end up carrying the weight of their father's absence. Maybe he knows he is safer here than he would be in South London.

These journeys, these quests, are very important, but more important still is to honour the feeling that you need to make them. To set out.

The single young woman pedalling hard up the hill with her belongings crammed into the bicycle packs slung over the back wheel is on her way as well. On this morning, on this road, it is a similar journey that links the three of us. What we have in common is that none of us know the outcome.

Walking with a stick or a pole means you have a hand on the earth to gauge just how deep the mud is, and a tool to bring the hanging blackberries down. Also, there is a natural genetic inheritance at work. There is a certain way that hunters carry their spear down at their side and, often on flatter walks, almost unconsciously, this is how the pole comes to be held.

Okehampton has positioned itself as 'the walking centre for Dartmoor.' So it is probably natural to assume that the town is chock-a-block with walking poles, thick socks and Kendal Mint Cake.

Once, on a walk in the Chilterns with some friends, none of us actually remembered 'the map', so we wandered into a newsagents and enquired whether they had any local maps. The man behind the counter looked over his glasses and said, 'It's strange, a lot of people come in here asking for maps but we never have any in.'

On any given day there are probably quite a few people wandering round the walking centre for Dartmoor enquiring about walking poles, but it seems they never have any of those in, either.

Fortune prevailed, however. There is a small collection of old bent-handled walking sticks in the antique shop on the corner at the end of town. They are curved-handled and thick to hold, meant for leaning on to ease the pain of dried-up hips and knees.

Having heard my explanation about the journey ahead, the man behind the counter says, 'Hang on there a minute,' and in due course returns with two well-travelled walking poles for the princely sum of five pounds. We shake hands.

⌃ 1,466 feet

Day Two

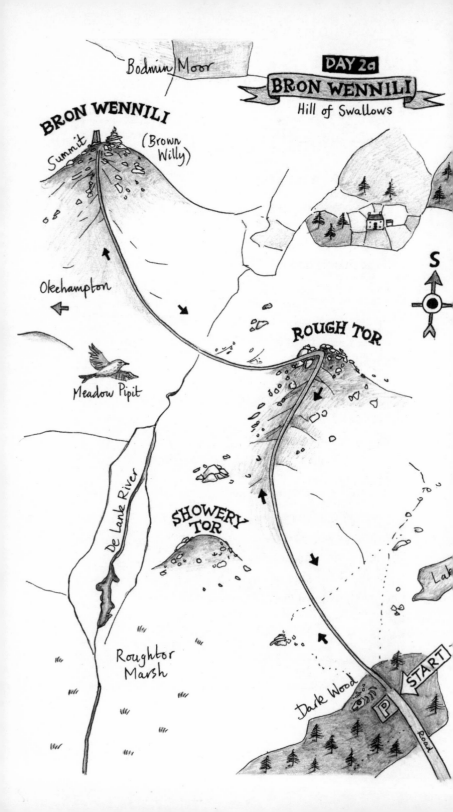

Bodmin Moor

DAY 2a

BRON WENNILI

Hill of Swallows

BRON WENNILI

Summit   (Brown Willy)

Okehampton

Meadow Pipit

ROUGH TOR

De Lank River

SHOWERY TOR

Roughter Marsh

Lak

START

Dark Wood

P

Road

S

Directions

Four and a half miles
Allow two hours

▷ This is not a difficult walk, but everything changes if the mist is down.

▷ There is a very good car park at the end of Rough Tor road, which becomes the straight road in. At the bottom of the car park is a stream with a bridge across it.

▷ From here, the path becomes vague, but it is best to head for the summit of Rough Tor as this allows for some extra height gain. Bronn Wennili (Brown Willy) is clearly visible from the summit of Rough Tor.

▷ Once you have reached the summit, head down to the base of the valley and towards a bridge that leads over a stream. There is a relatively good path on the other side of the bridge that will take you up onto the summit of Bronn Wennili.

Yes Tor and High Willhays, Dartmoor, Devon

The young woman sitting on the stony ground, leaning against the back wheel of a car, is breastfeeding her baby. She has her eyes closed, trying to glean some heat out of the sun. The air is cold. Under a leafless ash tree on the bank above her, an elderly man who walks painfully is holding a large yellow bucket and peering into the toilet storeroom.

Meldon Reservoir is seal-shaped. A strong southwesterly wind is ripping up the surface, pushing flocks of small waves against the machine-made wall to no avail. An almost overwhelming pall of melancholy hangs in the air. Not even the water falling and foaming down the front of the dam can make amends for what is drowned.

When human beings construct a reservoir we deconstruct an ecosystem, we create an emptiness. The natural world is in a state of constant movement, constant minute adjustment, tending to what is needed for everything to live with everything else – this is the creation of balance. It is a living force, this yearning for life, undescribed, not measured, this desiring, reaching and flowing. This is the cup that life is drinking from: an intelligence, a grace, that has formed the shapes of leaves, the colours of feathers, the pearlescence of shells.

To know this continual unfolding as cradled only within the certainties of gravitation, electromagnetism, strength and weakness is food for the dam. But to uphold the dark mantra of the survival of the fittest means that existence is only made possible by tragedy.

The light is sweet and clean, urging everything out of the ground. The path to Yes Tor follows the dam round then swings back on itself, cutting up the side of the hill onto a brow; the wind is fiercening.

The grass is almost grey here, broken and spent; the dead, dry stems laid out for the meadow pipits to forge into their hidden nests. Perfect circles held entirely by precisely placed straight stems, they are works of geometric art. The path splits and then splits again into an estuary in the grass, eventually losing all definition.

Walking without a path is much more of a feast for the senses; in woods this is especially the case. Large woods tend to have well-defined tracks and these will lead you through. But once you leave the path or the well-defined track you are no longer walking through the wood, you are walking in it, into it. Twenty yards in, your eyes adjust, your breathing deepens, your pace slows.

On the other side of the line of poles running underneath the Tor is the danger area – the army still uses this section of the moor for training exercises. There was no red flag flying from the Tor so it was safe to continue without being inadvertently shelled or shot at.

The flagpole on the summit of Yes Tor is beaten and rusted. It is more of an apparatus, a collection of pulleys and chains, almost a relic from the time before radio. Once there were men and women fluent in the alphabet of semaphore, speaking in flags, a flurry of words. This language was surely spoken here once.

There are perhaps prettier tors – Sharp Tor and definitely Luckey Tor – hidden in the twisting woods next to the sacred River Dart, a great grey cliff among the trees. It was hard to stand next to the flagpole and impossible to hear anything other than the wind.

Down from the summit there is enough rock to be just about protected from the wind; it is chaotic and angry above me, but quieter underneath, wrapped up and sealed in, alone. Not even the crows are flying.

High Willhays is the highest point in Britain south of the Brecon Beacons. It is a whole two yards closer to the sky than Yes Tor and it is a 10-minute walk along a ridge between the two. They are very different. High Willhays doesn't feel like an outpost, it is part of the moor rather than separate from it. A round mound of stones, some of them splattered with lichen: this would have been a better place to rest up.

There isn't a path to Black Tor. The ground is still wet but heading down, the wind is easing and the skylarks are beginning to emerge soundlessly from the grasses, flying low, not

wanting to be seen. On the ground they are quiet birds.

In Black Tor copse, oaks are growing out of boulders, everything is covered in a rough velvet of moss. The trunks, the branches, all even with green – this is the last wood before the moor, an enclave; there is no symmetry here. It is a steep descent through the trees from rock to rock, using branches as handholds. Each branch has been cast by the wind; they are as hard as bronze. This is a thin place, a doorway into another time.

The West Okement River running through the valley beneath the wood is young, innocent. By the time most rivers reach the coastal plains and cities they have become serious and stern; they are almost weary.

Once, going home over London's Chelsea Bridge, around 8 o'clock on an early May evening, the wind had whipped up the surface of the Thames, covering it with small white waves, all of them lit by a waning sun. For a short time it was as if the river was crammed with white flowers. On that evening the River Thames was a bride, not a father.

The West Okement River is a skipping boy, spinning and singing:

Always forever
Come what may
In the sunny sun
On a rainy day.

We walk together until we reach the wall where the wild land comes to an end. Here the river flows into the reservoir, into taps, into showers and cisterns, and here he lets go of my hand and is gone.

⌃ **2,729 feet**

Directions

Six and a half miles
Allow three hours

▷ Make sure that the army have not flagged off the moor on the day you plan to walk. You can find this information on the GOV.UK website by typing 'Dartmoor firing times' into a search engine.

▷ There is a very good car park at Meldon Reservoir, which is well signposted from Okehampton.

▷ From the car park, follow the access road down to the reservoir and then cross the reservoir wall. There is a gate at the end and then the track bears round to the right. Follow it round for about 300 yards, at which point you will see a path leading up the hill on your left. Take this path.

▷ Although the track looks well marked on the map, it seems to peter out after about a mile, and, rather like a river tributary, splits and narrows as it approaches the base of Yes Tor. The boundary here between the moor and firing range is a long curling line of poles. Once you are on the other side, so to speak, just follow your nose and the drier ground up onto Yes Tor.

▷ There is a very obvious path from Yes Tor to High Willhays that simply runs along the ridge between the two.

▷ From High Willhays, head north, walking down towards Black Tor but keeping to the left of the Tor itself. There is no path and the ground is boggy in places. Remember in springtime to keep an eye out for ground-nesting birds. The skylark will slip away quietly, flying about 20 yards or so, before apparently resting. The meadow pipit will feign injury to attract your attention away from the site of the nest. If you see these two birds, please change course immediately, giving the area from which they flew a wide berth (at least 50 yards).

▷ Just before the river valley the bank steepens into the quite enchanting Black Tor copse and beneath the copse is the River Oke.

▷ Simply follow the river down to the reservoir and take the path that runs along the south side of the water.

DAY 2b YES TOR & HIGH WILLHAYS

Skylark

Beaten & rusted flagpole

YES TOR
Summit

HIGH WILLHAYS

Okehampton Common

MOD
(Danger area)

(a bit boggy)

Across grass

BLACK TOR COPSE

Meadow pipit nest

Meldon Reservoir

West Okement River

Road

P

START

E
N ← → S
W

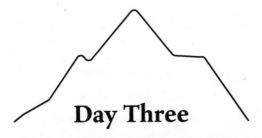

Day Three

Great Hangman and Holdstone Down, Devon

Music: 'Mr Lucky Goes Latin'
by Henry Mancini

There is a large red tanker in the bay in front of Combe Martin. It isn't moving. This means one of two things – either the captain is waiting for clearance to head up the Bristol Channel and into the docks, or he has cut the engines and is waiting out a storm.

The sky is thick and lowering, one solid layer of darkening cloud, and the sea is turning grey. The wind comes in sorties, lifting litter into the air along the high street and dropping it back down again. No one is smiling.

The car reeks: a heady scent of yesterday's vomit and dead foxes. It is the boots and socks; they were left outside last night but it is clear there is now no remedy – the boots must be letting in water. A fresh pair of socks might help. Yesterday's socks were almost solid this morning, like a couple of slabs of Camembert. Or they have simply died.

In the absence of a bin, cremation is the only option. It must have looked quite sinister, a car pulled up in a layby with a man sitting out from the driver's seat trying to set fire to some socks. The matches didn't even scald them, the lighter barely singed them; they are buried now.

The highest sea cliffs in the world lean against the island of Maui, rising up some 3,000 feet out of the Pacific Ocean. Great Hangman is the highest sea cliff in England, a rock face of 800 feet guarded by floating birds. It is also the highest point on the 630-mile South West Coast Path.

Everything is changing colour, folding inwards. The tension before storms holds a knowing that something will be changed irrevocably. It is the time spent once the house is tidied, the table set, the fire laid, waiting for her to arrive. Storms are meant to bring your house down. To lay waste to the garden, to breach the wall around your heart.

Blackthorn petals have fallen into confetti on the mud of the path leading up from Combe Martin. It runs through a hall of hissing trees to a porch and out beyond into a spring green field. Here, ewes are snugged in the dips of grass and up against field walls, lambs wrapped tight into their mother's fleeces. Some lambs will die tomorrow, mostly of pneumonia, once the storm is past.

Up towards Little Hangman the flurries come stronger and now the first blotches of rain hit the ground hard, and with each wave the intensity increases. Pulling up the hood of the waterproof means the sound of the rain on the Gore-Tex disturbs the relationship between what is heard and what is seen – the outside and the inside. Inside the Gore-Tex is a firing range of stones on paper. Rain is good for the hair.

The map is melting. It isn't one of those bulky plastic-coated water-resistant, expensive ones. Each time I look at it, run a finger over it, it disintegrates a little more and the way becomes less clear and really, in a beautiful storm, who needs a plastic folder hanging from their neck? Much better to be lost. There seem to be many paths up to Great Hangman – runnels through the heather which has turned black. The birds have all vanished.

The lost boys have taken the summit, arrived on the ship of the wind run aground. They are shouting as loud as their painted faces, dancing on the heather. This is a wild party, an incursion of mayhem – it is impossible to stand, I am forced to bow. Offshore the red tanker is blurred and rolling from side to side.

Rising in the northeast, Holdstone Down seems unaffected, apart. It is a still point, shrouded grey and graceful in the midst of all this noise. There was never an intention to go there, not until now.

The path down into the valley is wide and gently swings and curves through the heather, arriving at the corner of a wall and eventually reaching a small wood. It is quieter here under the storm and there are two young men who look almost dry sitting on some rocks next to the stream running along the valley floor. They both have beards and could easily be the strangers that change the route of the journey with a word, with a promise, waiting here at the bridge marking the point between two worlds.

The rain has not yet caught up with the stream, which strangely flows slowly, straining the last time it rained out of the hills. It won't take long to fill now that it is raining hard – maybe half an hour or so. On the way back it will be eager and rising.

On the other side of the bridge is a steep and slippery grassed slope leading up to a stony track. Holdstone Down is not on the South West Coast Path and the way is again unclear, ending in heather. In August this hill must be completely pink.

The summit is less rowdy, the sky is beginning to take on form and in the midst of this, three house martins come swerving in from the sea. They have slipped through a crack in the rain. They are heading for summer and once they arrive they will claim a piece of sky. They are made of air

and weigh slightly less than a stamped addressed envelope. And they carry with them the letters of proof that the long winter and the dark nights that tried to weave their need are truly waning. That it is time for the cow parsley to start to rise and the ponds to shine.

Tucked into the rain haze northwest beyond Holdstone Down is one of the smallest churches in England. I was there some time ago. Trentishoe church is more of a grotto, and like so many rural churches it is quietly being forgotten. With each passing year a thicker layer of silence settles.

The porch is little bigger than a cupboard, and inside a piece of scarlet velvet is draped over some tiny pews and the air smells of cake and make-believe. It is as if it is only ever used by children, and if you sat still enough for long enough they would emerge from the walls, and from under the pews dressed as pirates, lions and queens.

Back down on the valley floor, the stream has filled and a pair of wheatears are surveying the land. He is following her. Others might consider her plain, whereas he will do just about anything to keep her attention focused on him; it is his way of guarding her extraordinary beauty.

The two bearded young men must be making their way towards Combe Martin. Maybe they are talking or maybe they are walking in silence; either way, neither is alone.

Walking alone comes with a much higher risk of death. When we die while walking alone we are known as a 'lone walker'; this is especially true if we die far from home – that's how the local papers will report it. And it is true, many lone walkers do die on account of the wounds they are carrying at the time. They die of bereavement, they die seeking the cure for betrayal, from the dark velvet pain of lost love.

But there is another type of lone walker and they are not by and large courting solitude or healing, they are looking for a bridge to cross. It is, to a certain extent, a trade-off. This type of lone walker consciously exchanges insurance for enchantment. To cross the bridge requires the laying down of all wounds and all weapons.

The rain has stopped. Out on the horizon over the sea there is a white hem and the gulls are cornering low over the waves, feasting on the wind. Back in Combe Martin the town is waking up. It is three o'clock in the afternoon.

⋀ 4,901 feet

Directions

Six and a half miles
Allow three hours

▷ There is good parking in Combe Martin.
Essentially, it is a straight run out of the town
following the coast northeast and the coast path is
well marked. It is important to detour onto Little
Hangman in order to gain a few extra feet.

▷ From Great Hangman the coast path leads down
into a valley and a wooded area and over a stream.
You can follow the coast path up towards Holdstone
Down and then cut in from there, or you can make
your way up onto the summit with the crows, along
the many sheep paths.

▷ For the return journey, retrace your steps until
just before Little Hangman, where there is another
footpath on your left. This is not a madly interesting
path but it leads down to the outskirts of Combe
Martin and from here you just keep heading
downwards into the town.

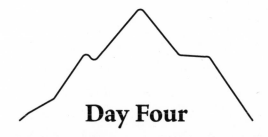

Day Four

Glastonbury Tor, Somerset

Music: 'Why?' by Mezzowave

The sun is cutting a line of light through the middle of the drawn curtains where they don't quite meet. I open them. A white-haired man is standing in the next-door-but-one garden, looking at the soil. The entire backyard is dug into an even tilth. There are two almost identical sections dissected by a concrete path that runs evenly between them and ends in front of a wooden shed that takes up most of the back wall.

There is much to be learned from observing the soil. He is assessing his digging, noticing the colour of the earth. Maybe today, this afternoon, once the sun has been on it, he will rake it over; the final part of the process of preparation.

He won't plant immediately, he will let the soil settle for a couple of days. He will watch the weather forecast, look at the sky and wait for a morning, a day or a night full of rain. The seedlings will be planted and the first lines of seeds sown 12 hours before the rain arrives. Over this period, which could be a week or so, he will be memorising this section of soil. And each morning, if you were to ask him, he would be able to point to exactly where the blackbird has crossed, where the jay has briefly landed. He is tending this small piece of land, and on this planet at this point in time, that casts him as a romantic hero.

All of Glastonbury is closed. Yesterday's rain has washed the place clean and the early sun is drying the pavements. There is no bustle, just the occasional car. The church halfway up the high street is muted, has chosen the right to remain silent, and will not dance with Jack o' the Green, or sit in the deep woods in a circle with witches. Here, more than any other place in England, it is so very clear that the woad and the word have yet to make peace.

The sun is beginning to lean into the day. Fairies stare and crystals pulse from every other shop window leading up the hill towards the top of town; the Green Man is ever present. He is almost permeable, in a constant state of osmosis flowing between changing angles of light, rolling petals into his skin and drinking the rain. He is a sadhu and perhaps there were once many of them wandering between Ireland and Russia, not needing bread nor bound to patronage, walking into Eden at will.

On the back road leading to the base of the Tor, the door to the white spring is shut; it is still early. Inside is a shrine to candlelight and water

– picked and twisted sticks forming doorways into sanctuaries.

No one speaks, it is a place of whispers, which in turn become falling water. There is not a soul on the top of the Tor and barely a breeze. The sun is now horizontal to the tower, carving out the doorway into a buttress of light. It is hard not to project meaning and purpose into these stones, to bring out the dead.

There is an absence here. It seems the Tor has always been set apart: a place of lightning, a place raising all that craves resolution to hear the still, small voice there in the eye of the storm, but in the sunlight this morning it is as if something is being stretched; the walls are being thinned.

The present is simply the meeting point between the past and the future. In that sense everything is held within it, it is utterly dynamic, it is where all points meet.

Maybe the elderly gentleman is drinking his morning cup of tea now; he had the air of a widower. Perhaps he is sitting down in a kitchen that is as neat as his garden with the radio on, tuned to the local station. And laid out just behind his cup is some of the seed he saved from last year. Seeds are time capsules. There is a garden waiting in each one of them.

⌃ **5,295 feet**

Directions

Two miles
Allow one hour

▷ It is best to do this walk first thing in the morning.

▷ To achieve the required height gain it is important to start right at the bottom of the town, just down from the town hall.

▷ From here, follow the high street up to the top and here turn right. This road essentially leads above the grounds of Glastonbury Abbey and then passes the delightful Chalice Well gardens on the left.

▷ Just past Chalice Well, take the road on your right, which leads past the entrance to the White Spring on your right.

▷ Keep going for another half mile or so and the footpath for the base of the Tor is there on your right.

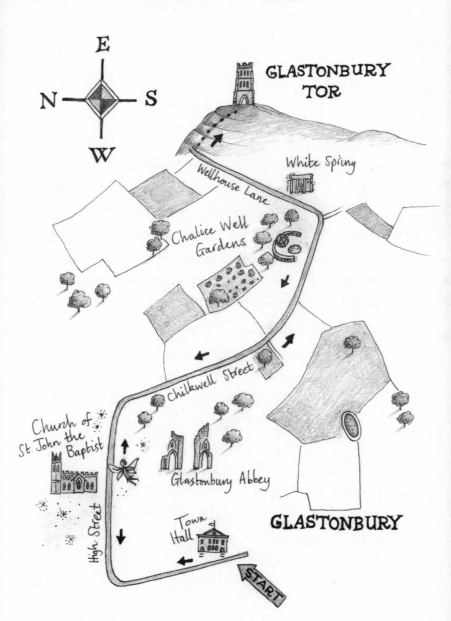

DAY 4a GLASTONBURY TOR

E
N · S
W

GLASTONBURY
TOR

White Spring

Wellhouse Lane

Chalice Well
Gardens

Chilkwell Street

Church of
St. John the
Baptist

Glastonbury Abbey

GLASTONBURY

High Street

Town
Hall

START

Cheddar Gorge to Beacon Batch, Somerset

The only redemption for the car is *Palo Santo*, Spanish for 'sacred stick'. It burns with a sweet smoke. The fresh socks are not working. The boots are sodden on the inside – water is leaching in, flowing from the thick and dew-soaked morning grass. There is a whole ecosystem thriving in both of them, feasting on sweat, water and warmth, a mire in the making.

It is a predominantly straight road across the levels from Glastonbury to Cheddar. The houses are small, hunched, it is a 'Mal area'. Rather like the fens, another drained land, the levels are not sugar lump England.

Before insecticides you would, in the summer, have been endlessly bitten and in the winter there is no lull in the cold wind and no wood for the fire – there is an absence of trees both here and on the Fens. The pheasants are scrawny, eking out an existence on the margins of the fat fields. The only break in the pall of poverty is one brimstone butterfly dancing to the score of spring.

Cheddar is almost alpine, houses huddled against the base of rising grey cliffs. The light is made from the same source that illuminates the Samaria Gorge in Crete. It is compressed, somehow magnified, reaching deep into the small, clear river; turning luminous the ribbons of weed gently swaying in the water that runs out through the gorge.

The water gardens are quite lovely. I wish I had arrived earlier, before the shops and cafes opened. This place feels Edwardian or Victorian, completely different to Glastonbury. At some point it must have been invaded by men wearing plus fours and sporting an array of large moustaches. And there they stand with coils of rope over their shoulders looking up into the rock.

It was the British Empire that decided that mountains needed to be climbed and cliff faces scaled. Cheddar would have been the ideal training ground before heading off for the Matterhorn and the Eiger, where a fair few people of this era died. And yes, it was predominantly about 'conquering' or taming the wild. The trouble was, some of those who set out to 'conquer' fell in love and then they reverted, shaking off all that had been tamed in them. The sons and daughters of the owners of the dark satanic mills that furnished them with enough money to wander or to climb returned, half suspecting that the point was, in fact, to be overcome by the mountain or rendered quiet by the slipping stream.

Conquering is a dreadful business, a blighted gene. I want nothing to do with it, nothing to do with conquering space, defacing the wilderness with a flag. Climbing up, walking to the summit, is a calling, a summoning, for what can only be known, seen and heard on the edge of the land and the sky and in the space between them.

There is a dog – something between a Labrador and a lurcher – smiling between the planks of a wooden gate. She or he is wagging their tail. The smaller West Highland terrier is not so welcoming, covered in earth, an inch away from growling.

It is good to be walking through a wood. The light is moving the stones on the path and the trees begin to thin into single hawthorns before the summit. I can hear the road but I cannot see it.

The group of Danish bikers who were drinking tea and eating biscuits outside one of the cafes must be driving through now, a machine at a time, a one-minute route through a mountain. The highest point in Denmark is just over 558 feet and there are no gorges. The man who stops at the back of the family group on its way up really wants to talk, but is so out of breath he barely manages a sentence.

The road at the bottom must have started as a path and evolved into a cart track before it was metalled. It is a pity it is here at all. It is not only the light that is compressed in gorges, the sound too is cleaner, the birdsong does not dissipate as fast, and gorges are havens from the wind; they store silence.

There is no footpath through this gorge, it has been captured by cars – they patrol this sunken street. So the essential gift of the gorge is lost; the essence is compromised, blurred by engines. Perhaps for a couple of days a year the road might be closed and the gorge walked, the silence revived.

It must be spring. There is one comma butterfly on the path leading up towards Beacon Batch. The entrance onto the heath is flooded, there must be at least a foot of water separating a green spring field from a land very much still in winter. There are shades of Christmas here, the grass is almost icing-white and underfoot the black earth is moist, the colour of raisins. Horses have made the paths through this tundra, they run vaguely between the colourless heather to small patches of eaten grass. The boots are drenched.

Day Four

From the summit, the two suspension arms of the Severn Bridge are rising in the northwest with the rough urban symmetry of Bristol before them. And there is Glastonbury Tor – a bump in the east.

It is crowded here, almost a party: mountain bikers, hikers, casual walkers, and a very young teenage couple who have clearly bunked off school and had the bright idea of wandering all the way up here so they can be alone. Beacon Batch is not a kissing hill. Everyone is simultaneously eating sandwiches; it is as if a whistle was blown and we all opened our lunch boxes at the same time. There is no litter and very little conversation; we are all sitting, chewing and staring into the distance.

Spring has arrived. The air is heating up. Heading down on an ever-widening black earth path, a posse of flies are sunning themselves on the rocks lining the edge. At this time of year they are quick, like shooting stars. This is the advance party, by midsummer they are slow, drunk and careless.

Then, emerging into a wood, a horse gallops through the trees; it is chestnut with a flowing blond mane and yet strangely it leaves no hoofprints. I bend to look at the ground, searching for signs, and there is nothing; not a leaf has been moved. It was definitely here.

The line of elderly men and women carrying buckets, crowbars and spades are volunteers. Their work is done – a gleaming new aluminium gate stands opposite the one they must have put in last week. Their passing advice is not to manhandle the gate too harshly as the cement won't have dried yet.

Thirsty stems of grass are coming up through the concrete and tar at the gates of the Tuttors Hill Quarry; there is only half a noticeboard and on the other side of the large padlocked fence is a bruised building.

This place has an air of exhaustion. The quarry is exhausted, that's the term that's used, and a pall of heavy energy hangs in the air. It is an abandoned land, it has become a tomb, and even in the bright sunshine it is cold to pass. It isn't the lamenting of the reservoir; here is more the scent of something dishonoured.

Do not pity the quarry, it will recover in time, seeds will land, flowers return, birds nest. Pity the desolation of the ruthless heart that lays waste to the garden and cannot mourn the loss.

There is a peacock butterfly on the road, signalling spring. Now that there is some warmth in the sun the land is preparing for a party. In Cheddar the tourists are wearing sleeveless shirts and the river has turned into a sea pool, gin clear, the strands of green weed swaying.

There is a hippo bone that was found in one of the caves in a display cabinet at the back of the shop selling tickets for tours of Wookey Hole. There is nowhere to sit, apart from on some steps leading down to the river. A small group of young women, all with dyed, straightened hair, file past eating ice cream. It is strange, the horse in the wood made no sound. It was silent as it galloped between the trees.

︿ **7,756 feet**

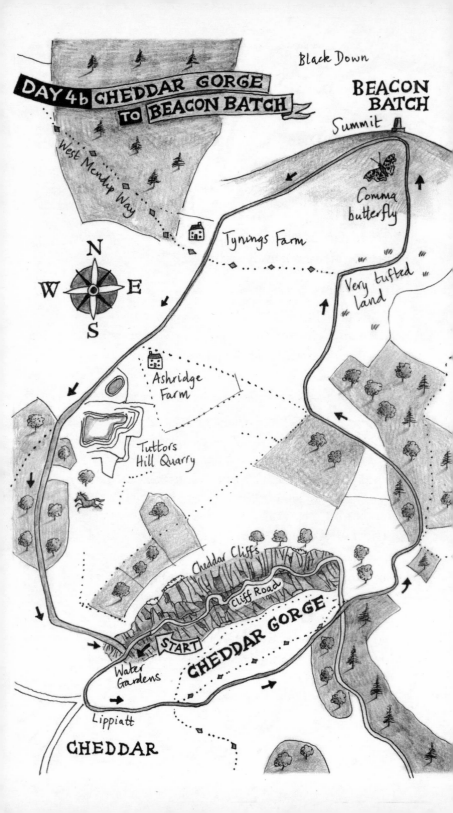

Directions

Ten and a half miles
Allow four hours

▷ Try to park in Cliff Road. (To find a space you will
need to arrive relatively early in the day.)

▷ Walk back down Cliff Road, passing the river
gardens, until you reach the Black Dog Saloon.
Here turn left and follow a road named the Lippiatt
for about 100 yards. The path you need to take is
then on your left and this path leads up through the
woods onto the ridge above Cheddar Gorge.
As the wood begins to thin, you will reach the
highest point above the gorge and now the path
begins to descend, at some points quite steeply,
until you reach the road running through the
bottom of the gorge.

▷ The path you need is directly on the other side of
the road and this leads gently upwards, passing an
abandoned quarry pool on your left before running
along the base of a grassy valley which ends in an
intersection of four paths. Take the path in front of
you, which is effectively the middle path out of the
three. The one on the left is the Mendip Way and

the one on the right leads to the beautifully named Velvet Bottom.

▷ This path runs to fields and passes through a small patch of woodland. As this woodland begins to run out, there is another intersection of four paths. Again, take the middle path and this will lead you to the base of the enclosure that holds Black Down and Beacon Batch.

▷ The horses have made their own paths through this very tufted land, so you can weave your way to the summit along these or follow the edge of the rough ground around to your right and join up with the main path, which will take you to the summit.

▷ From the summit, take the path south, passing Tynings Farm and onto the minor road leading to Ashridge Farm. Having passed the farm, take the path on your right. This runs higgledy piggledy through a couple of fields and the new iron gates, then onto a piece of corrugated iron which has 'Path' and a very helpful arrow painted onto it.

Day Four

▷ This path will lead you downhill and into the wood and, after about 500 yards, onto the quarry road, where you turn right. This road will take you all the way back into Cheddar.

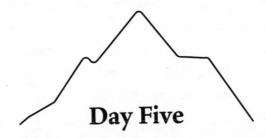

Day Five

Crickley Hill, Gloucestershire

Music: 'Food For My Soul' by The Dragons

Red and raw down to the blood: three toes on the left foot and one on the right. These are not blisters, they are sores born in the dank bacteria-ridden interior of the sodden boots. The toes are bandaged in blister packs but this cannot go on, otherwise infection will set in. It is time for a new pair of boots.

Nurseries of new leaves hang over the bridleway. They are all translucent; most of the sunlight goes straight through them and they are glowing green. This is tenderness. Running down through the bed of stones in the bridleway, which is rising steeply, is a small stream. This hill is still letting water from the storm two days ago.

The flies are gathering force, calling in a crescendo before falling silent for 30 seconds or so. One fly can fill a room with the sound of its wings. This heat is a healing from the scouring of winter, bringing fish up from the depths of ponds and lakes to slide the surface. The summer travellers are now beginning to arrive – whitethroats, warblers – and on the coast gannets and puffins are making landfall after their winter at sea.

The shade is thickening. Along the ridge the canopy sinks from high pines into old clumps of coppiced hazels. The earth is still wet here, the mud black, soft as potter's slip and unable to hold the prints of strangers and dogs.

Once the summit was a village; it is now a meeting point. The cafe sells postcards and lemonade and on the display boards are drawings of neolithic homes and an illustration of a bearded man wearing the skins of animals. He shared this hill with bears and wild cattle and lived hearing a very different soundtrack – at dusk, wolves – and from within the woods that stretched as far as the eye could see, into the beyond where Gloucester now stands, constant birdsong filling the still mornings. Now it is engines, emergencies, the growling of machines.

Did he live his life in a hurry, sell the birds and the silence for flints?

To whom do the birds belong?

⋀ 8,543 feet

Directions

Two and a half miles
Allow one hour or so

▷ Heading north on the A46, just before the Cheese Rollers Inn in Shurdington, is a small lane on your right called Greenway Lane. Head up here. There are a few places to park.

▷ Follow the bridleway to just before the ridge, and here take the marked footpath on your right. This footpath leads all the way along the ridge to the Crickley Hill Country Park visitor centre, where there is a cafe.

▷ From the cafe, walk through the car park and take the path heading directly down the hill. This leads over fields and ends up towards the bottom of Greenway Lane.

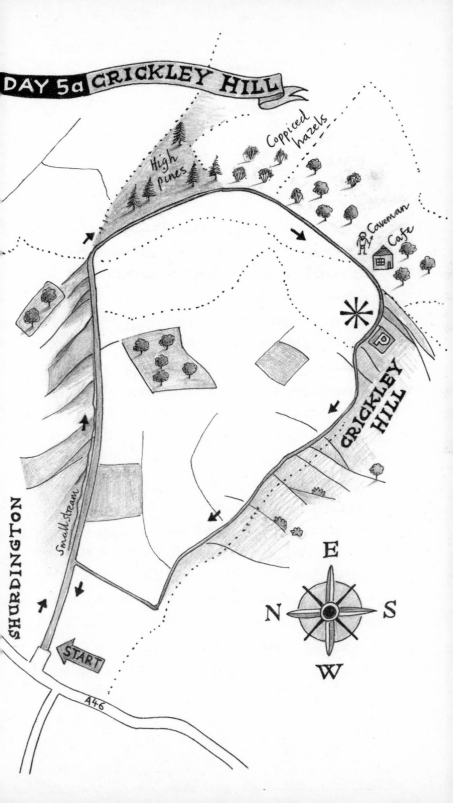

Cleeve Hill, Gloucestershire

An elderly couple are sitting in the front seats of their round red car; both doors are open. They sit in silence as they eat their sandwiches. There isn't much of a view from the car park. It is almost encased in banks of earth and the ground is dry and dusty. The sky is a pure blue, spring blue; it is young, newborn – that is the gift.

It seems as if everyone who was on Crickley Hill has been summoned to Cleeve Hill; they are not that far from each other. Middle-aged women are walking dogs of different sizes and there's the occasional retired man, one in a pastel blue peaked cap and shorts the same colour as his legs. It is the sunlight that is making them smile.

As the path leads down between two high hedges a cuckoo pumps the air. This is a statement of intent: the first one of the year. These notes, fattened in Africa and carried north over the Sahara, are now playing on an English hill: the sweet voice of deception. The changeling child arrives in the warmth of an innocent house. It kills the children already there and steals the crown of love. As the 14th-century Persian poet Hafez has written, 'learn to recognise the counterfeit coins'.

At the bottom of the valley a spring is flowing from within a small dome of Victorian stone built into a steep-sided field. An arc of water dives into an overflowing trough. Maybe it is such a calming sound because the human heart is 73 per cent water. The two horses standing right in the middle of the path up against the wall are in a state of high relaxation; they stand with their eyes closed. At this time of year the flies haven't yet mustered to bother the horses' lips and eyes. We have a little chat, they don't move. Why should they?

There isn't exactly a path that leads up from the farm at the bottom of the valley. Everything is in bud here, just becoming. And beyond the far gate is another valley and rising on either side are paths running in small ridges above pits and hollows where limestone has been extracted. Here there is a mixture of a very thin layer of grass and fine rubble.

On the far side of the valley a young couple are kissing on a bench placed in front of a pool made from damming a small stream. The sun is hidden on this north side of the hill and emerges at the top of a short, steep climb.

In the distance is a single backlit tree and there are shapes of human beings: women, pushchairs and children. They are silhouetted, spreading blankets and leaning over bags.

It isn't the summit. The summit they say is another half mile eastwards. This tree is the highest in the Cotswolds and for £500 you can have your name rendered on a brass plaque attached to the circular wall that surrounds it. It is pretty much the only tree up here and the land feels as if it holds very few flowers, they have been smothered. It is tired land.

The summit is a concrete trig point barely two yards from the fence behind it. It isn't a restful place, not somewhere to sit and be. It isn't a destination, it feels alone, as if very few people have placed their hands on top of it. There isn't dreaming or healing here, nothing is being reached for or resolved. It is a glass without wine. Maybe it is the two towering metal masts just before it, or that it is just up from a car park, but it is strange to be on a summit where there is a complete absence of celebration, where not one vote is cast for dancing.

The women and children by the memorial tree are preparing to leave. It was a short picnic; blankets are being folded and Tupperware boxes stashed under pushchair seats. The sky is warm now, the water bottle is empty and the day is sliding into late afternoon.

This is the last of the southern hills. It is not so much a land that is known, it is the echoes of home that it holds – the colour of the rivers, how often it rains, the familiar mix of birds. It isn't actually a gradual change, there are in fact so many lines that

are drawn across this island and so many different islands within it.

Some of these islands are small areas containing maybe only a handful of one type of bird. And there are lines beyond which white admiral and purple emperor butterflies do not live. Each piece of land, each hill, each river, will hold a slightly different mix of life. Different soil types mother different flowers. But what is less apparent is the change of light: a slightly different angle of the sun overhead means the land is differently lit. Maybe this cannot be named, that it is simply experienced as the knowing of the tender grass of home.

As a stranger it is easy to lose your bearings in Cheltenham, which is sweltering. Cities are cages, where we live in herds and shoals, and they are loud: engines, sirens, drills and music. There is surely no other species that takes over so completely. Maybe ants operate in the same way, creating fortresses, their own micro-environments. They too have boundaries, nationalities, and they fight wars, red killing black, black killing brown. They are tribal.

Inside the shop this micro-environment seems shaded, almost subdued; rows of single boots each on their own shelf stuck to the walls, trays of newly minted blue and purple water bottles, posters of young human beings either sitting happily in heather or standing on an outcrop with the mist below them. In here it never rains.

Human beings started wearing shoes some 35,000 years ago. This particular pair of mine must have trodden many, many thousands of miles but the rubber seam where the sole meets the leather is now completely degraded, there is hardly any of it left, and that is where the water is leaching in, soaking the socks.

The new boots are exactly the same as the old boots but they are dry on the inside. The sales assistants are straight out of school, there is not a wrinkle between them. He is tall and too quiet for the new tattoo on his arm. He will not smile, he moves quietly. She is only half here, she is enduring. The probabilities state that I will not see them again.

⌃ 9,478 feet

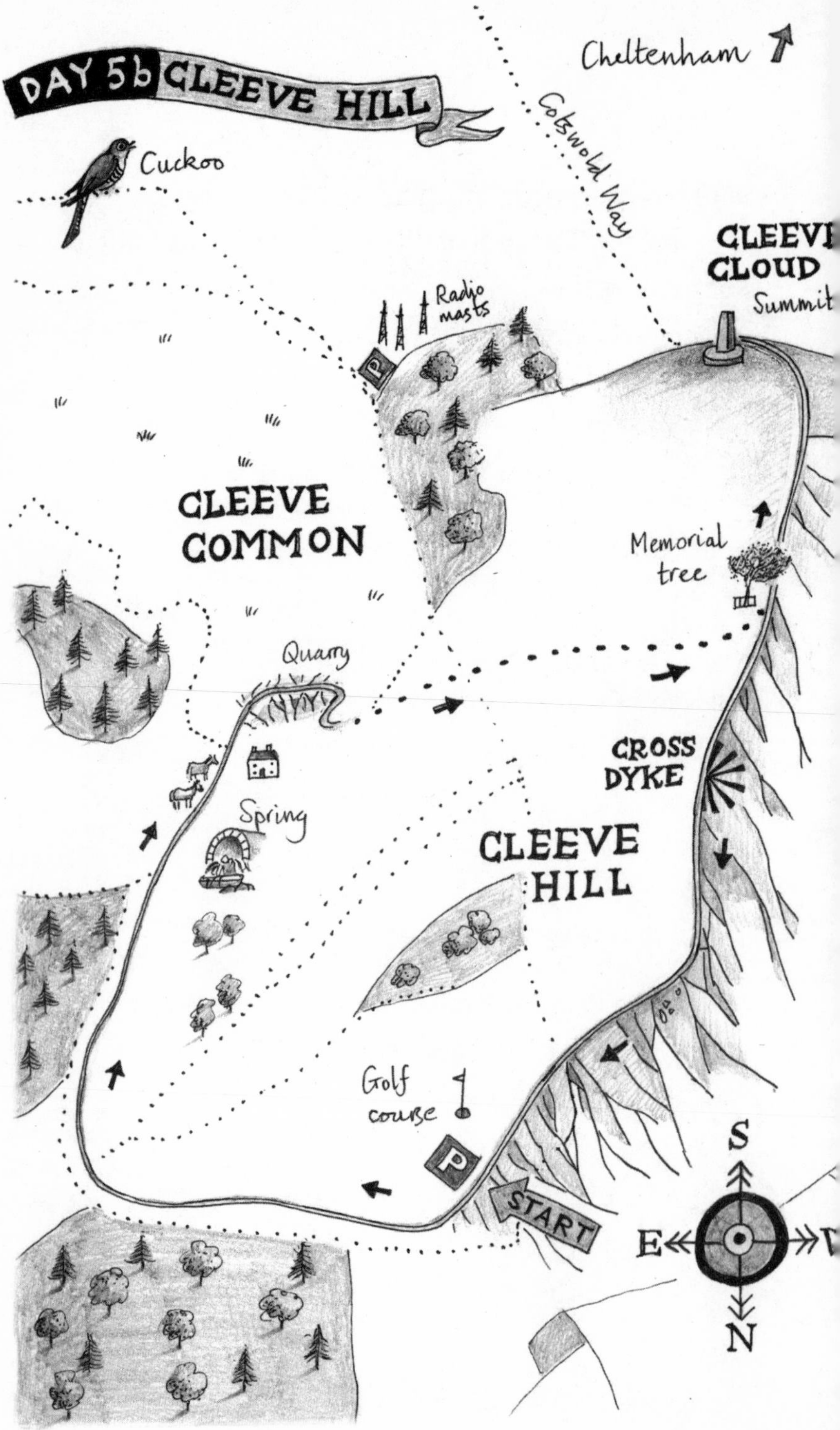

DAY 5b CLEEVE HILL

Cuckoo

Cheltenham

Cotswold Way

CLEEVE CLOUD
Summit

Radio masts

P

CLEEVE COMMON

Memorial tree

Quarry

Spring

CROSS DYKE

CLEEVE HILL

Golf course

P

START

S
E
N

Directions

Four and a half miles

Allow two and a half hours

▷ There is good public parking beyond the Cleeve Hill Golf Club.

▷ From the car park, head east along the wide track that leads down through a copse to the spring in the field. From here, follow the footpath around the farm, which will lead you back onto the common once again. Here I took a rough, steep path up through the abandoned quarries and then headed west over the common to the Memorial Tree.

▷ From the Memorial Tree, bear left over the common for about a mile and this will take you past a car park on your right and then two yards further on is the really very dour summit of Cleeve Hill.

▷ To return to the car park, simply follow the ridge all the way back, passing the Memorial Tree as you go.

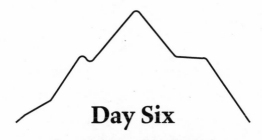

Day Six

The Malvern Ridge, West Midlands

Music: 'Corcovado' by Stan Getz and João Gilberto

The clouds descended in the night, the sky coming to rest, to sleep, on the earth. At three in the morning every street and every tree in Malvern would have been dreaming in a bed of mist. Now the few remnant strands that are left are running home. Here there is no border between the hill and the town, it is as if they merge, they belong to one another. It is almost a bridleway at the top of Pump Street leading upwards, it seems, over the roofs.

Just beneath Sugarloaf Hill, Shirley is holding a plastic bag and bending down, inspecting the path. She explains that her quarry is worms for her koi carp. They live perhaps in a small dug pond that sits just beyond the patio, they may well have been her late husband's passion. He would fuss over them, especially when he found it hard to communicate what he was feeling.

The conversation would run out of steam. He wouldn't leave the room immediately, he would stay seated just where he was and place his eyes back on the newspaper, but he wasn't reading, he was waiting, waiting for a natural lull, a gap, then he would rise and make his way quietly out through the back door and go and stand over the fish.

After the funeral the fish became just one more thing she had to deal with and she would go and stand next to them, wondering whether to sell them; to put an ad online. They began to share her thoughts and sometimes, when everyone else believed the grieving was over, her tears as well, falling into the water. Now the fish take care of her.

Everything is shining. The mist has left a dew thick enough to kneel in and run your hands through the grass and drink; more than enough to wash in. It is warm, this flush of air that has crept up from the south. It must be near 70 degrees and it is just past nine in the morning.

These hills are scribbled with paths. On the Ordnance Survey map it looks as if a child has drawn all over the slopes around Worcestershire Beacon with one green pencil. And it is busy, no one is ambling, women in lycra are running for the top and a boy is pushing hard on the pedals, refusing to let the gradient beat him. The shared mantra is 'Good morning'. The paths are the legacy of a health craze. The Victorians would turn up and take the waters leaching from the side of the hills and part of that healing was a morning or an evening constitutional. They have left their thoughts.

Worcestershire Beacon has been claimed for Queen Victoria, her name emblazoned on a diminutive column sitting on several layers of

forthright hexagonal stone. It is built to stand the test of time, the winds and the winter rains, solid and certain, but the birds seem to shun it. It is alien, stranded and utterly impervious to the present, it is an imposition.

From here the path runs west, one ambling line over the waves of each hill. End Hill, North Hill, Table Hill, Sugarloaf Hill, Worcestershire Beacon, Summer Hill, Perseverance Hill, Jubilee Hill, Pinnacle Hill, Black Hill, British Camp, Millennium Hill, Hangman's Hill, Swinyard Hill, Midsummer Hill, Raggedstone Hill and finally Church End Hill.

The air is completely clear now and they say you can see 15 counties from here. It is a perfect 360-degree view, really the first one there has been. These hills rise up from the surrounding plain which encircles them and at some point I must have crossed the line between two worlds, entered the grove and emerged into a clearing.

The dividing line is some way beyond the reach of roads, where they come to an end, beyond the sound of individual cars and where the fields give out. This only happens in England, where the steep-sided slopes set in, or deep in a wood. From up here the plain is an underworld. The grind of machines, the lament of sirens, tied dogs barking. It is clearly a production system, a multiplicity of factory settings or logarithms, of codes all now generating the speed and the direction of travel.

It is such a clear run, this path etched along the ridge, it is almost a yellow brick road. Now, with the first flush of heat, it is dry along the top with an easy breeze. There is something of childhood here, new as spring, all crammed onto one small blanket drinking weak lemon squash out of blue plastic cups, raising up into the present faces of boys and girls, our small hands and the scent of salad cream. Surely this is a day for skipping.

The elderly woman dressed in a thick knitted cardigan is being pushed in a wheelchair as far as the section of metalled path will take her. She, too, it would seem, has slipped the bonds of adulthood. She tells me what a beautiful morning it is, as her eyes jump from the hills to the sky and back again. And she is impatient. Maybe it was her daughter who issued her and the young woman in a red T-shirt pushing her up the path with a list of instructions: 'Don't get cold. Don't go too far. Stay on the path. Don't go near water,' echoes reminding her of what it feels like to run free.

The sand martins are on their way to somewhere else. Fine small brown and cream birds made of velvet, they are clearly passing through, shooting the ridge just down from Summer Hill, heading for a wall of hard sand in which, at the end of a small tunnel, the female will lay three to five polished white eggs.

It is rare to see a bus stop with pink painted wooden panels held in three yellow frames. There is no graffiti. It is almost a pavilion; something you would find on the seafront of Brighton or Llandudno to keep off the rain and it is hard to imagine it was once new. This one in Upper Wyche surely had a grand opening; a brass band and a portly mayor with thick fingers squeezed into the scissors to cut the green ribbon.

From the top of Perseverance Hill one lone runner disappears into the trees that sit in the valley before the ascent onto Jubilee Hill and now, for the first time, there is no one else. The exercise hour must have passed. Maybe it is the unbroken sunlight, the overflowing warmth, that this is the word spoken and understood by bark and stems to release the petals and the leaves and wake the peacock butterflies.

This path is beautiful. It is held and strangely enclosed. The mania of the plain gives out to wooded slopes that seem to guard the open ground above them, and flowing neatly along the ridge is one sweet winding line, rising and descending south. It just takes time before the door opens into the garden, to arrive in the running of spring – the currency is wonder.

Here every colour, every movement, is happening for the first time, there are no repeating patterns. The door lies beyond need, beyond all the walls of certainty and the suffocations of security; the yearning for a castle. These are the counterfeit coins, they will be heavier tomorrow. They weigh the journey down.

The Malvern Hills Hotel is white and almost alpine. Once it must have been somewhere out of the way to honeymoon, to dress for dinner. It sits in the base of the pass between Black Hill and British Camp. Maybe in autumn it comes to life, when the fire is lit, when the wind knocks at the windows.

Perhaps there are no more than a handful of men and women alive now who can look back to the first time together, as she lay in his arms, delighting in the scent of his skin.

How she walked towards the bed and, not wanting to scare her, how he hardly dared to look. He saw her hand, her fingers, turning off the bedside light and in the dark heard the sound of her dressing gown as it fell onto the carpet. She left him five years later, they both remarried. But now, as he sits in a small modern conservatory, he is the last one alive and he is not strong enough any more to quell this memory of how he loved completely then. He can hold it for hours, that moment when there were no stars, no seas, not even the fields of home.

Just further on from the hotel, Sally's Place is alive with crockery and the clatter of conversation. The tables are next to the road under umbrellas, there are different coloured cakes, some on stands, others on plates, and a wall of postcards: the hills in snow and the dresses of autumn. There is no door to go through, this is English street food, sugar and wheat. Not really the best fuel for the climb up to British Camp, where the earth is dug into circular ditches and banks. These are scars bearing the memories of mistrust, attack and what remains unforgiven. It is a good place to fly kites, to roll down the banks, to drink cider.

No one else is walking on. There is a small gathering on the summit but the path running south to Midsummer Hill is empty. Slowly it would seem the hills are lowering and while each one requires an ascent, it is slightly lower than the one before and the murmuring plain moves ever closer. Last year's bracken is still folded over

Day Six

the ground in bronze strands, dried and cracked underneath Swinyard Hill.

The climb up through the Gullet is still muddied and the stones are wet beneath the trees. No one stops in Hollybush. The cars come over the brow on the one road every so often but it is strangely solitary, this place that everyone else is driving through.

Raggedstone Hill is steep. I have run out of water. The even path that began in Malvern, so certain and wide enough for a queen, has thinned, become rutted, with brambles reaching across it. There are blind corners in the low scrub and now clumps of primroses tucked along the edges, a suspicion of foxes – that is usually all they leave. Then round another bend, blackthorn branches crammed with white blossoms: the flowers before the leaves. This silk and scented skin now uncovered, giving milk to the sky, letting honey down.

Whiteleaved Oak is almost hidden; it is stumbled upon. A row of the smallest houses in England. Here, the path almost vanishes under an old copse, wandering out into a field, rising round some hawthorns to the final trig point, Chase End Hill.

A middle-aged couple arrive from another direction, and while we are agreeing that there have been very few brimstone butterflies this year, a female flies just beneath us. Following her is a butter-yellow male; they are dancing.

It is essentially a descent, this walking day. A journey into quietness, from the town to the farm, from the leaf to the root. Heading down from a summit is often much more silent, simply because there is no destination. This is the door to wandering; the wanderer is not constrained by time, there is no route, no map, and like love, once you have been through this door it is not possible to return to where you started from.

⋀ 12,791 feet

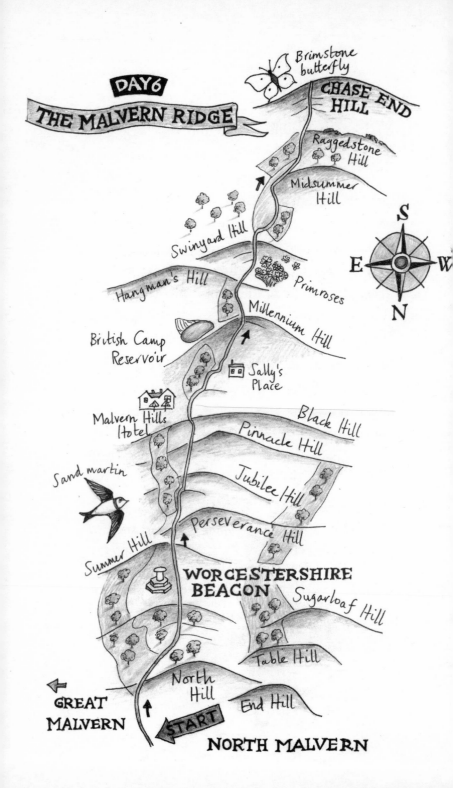

Directions

Ten miles

Allow four and a half hours

▷ There are a number of ways leading up onto the ridge from Malvern. I took the path at the top of Pump Street. This path zigzagged up to Worcestershire Beacon. From here, the route consists of one path heading west that crosses a couple of roads before reaching Hollybush.

▷ Here, turn right and walk down past the bus stop on the left. The continuing path is on the left: the path that heads straight up the hill, not the one which meanders off to the right. This straight path leads through the woods, up what is a steep incline and then down to Whiteleaved Oak.

▷ The final section of the path, up onto Chase End Hill, can be found just past the village noticeboard. There is a driveway that is also a right of way and this leads up through a small section of wood and out onto the trig point on Chase End Hill.

▷ The return to Malvern is best done by walking back to Hollybush. There is a very attractive path which cuts around the side of Raggedstone Hill and leads back to the meandering path near the bus stop. From here, it is either the bus or a taxi ride back into Malvern.

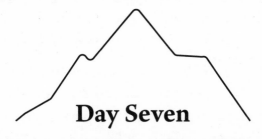

Day Seven

Caer Caradoc, Shropshire

Music: 'Like It Is' by Yusef Lateef

A lone carp is dreaming just beneath the surface of the second pond under Caer Caradoc hill: fish sleep suspended in water. He is swaying slowly from side to side, not quite a shadow, more of a spirit moving through the branches of the trees reflected on the water.

It is 7 o'clock in the morning and the fields are drenched in dew. Lambs and their mothers have gathered under an old oak where the grass is shorter. It won't be long before the sun dries the field – the sky is pure blue.

Most of the resident birds are now married for the season. Very few pairs stay together for life. Bullfinches, jackdaws and mute swans commit; to have and to hold, to love and to cherish, till death do us part. For the others, new research shows that there's a lot of hopping around going on, with many fledglings not being raised by their biological father. The chaos of courtship sparks again each spring, the males singing and dancing, the females deciding.

Male greater spotted woodpeckers 'drum', drilling into a suitable branch, one that will transmit sound, and from January up until June single males can drum up to 600 times a day. Really they are tropical birds painted black, red and white. Now, as the new leaves are arriving, they seem more at home; in winter they appear to be lost. The pair in the wood just beyond the pond leave together, swerving through the trees then out into the open beneath the western flank of the hill, heading into another world.

This morning there is fear without, it would seem, reason. The path is vague, just a series of dents in the earth, leading upwards. It is hardly unsafe, there is nothing to fear, nothing to do but walk up. The fear comes from what is being carried, what lies within.

The poet Rilke wrote in a letter to a certain Mr Kappus,

> *A man taken out of his room and, almost*
> *without preparation or transition, placed*
> *on the heights of a great mountain range,*
> *would feel something like that: an unequalled*
> *insecurity, an abandonment to the nameless,*
> *would almost annihilate him.*

Yes, this beating heart that comes with no guarantees, the sweetest strings that have been broken and buried, the empty cellars. All this, shaken and woken.

On Everest, death stalks every climber. Now, after a week of this walking, up, every day, into silence, it is all that has died and not been buried or has not been laid to rest smothered in routine or dragged around to parties. What was left in the storm, abandoned on the ledge, waiting for

us to return – who and what they hold come out shivering now, rising to the surface, freed from the self-inflicted bonds of routine. These are the drummers needing to be heard.

From the ridge, it looks as if the land has been washed. It is almost a straight valley that runs between Caer Caradoc and the Shropshire hills, straight enough for a railway line and one long road. The cars are silent from here, the train shines and glides. There isn't much of a path and there can be no good reason why Three Fingers Rock has acquired the name: something out of a Western, a place to meet at noon. The English tend not to do rocks, they are out at sea.

It is a gentle climb over grass up to the summit, there is a quietening breeze, the pall of morning still hanging over Church Stretton and above the town a blue sky and the green and yellow Shropshire hills.

⋏ **13,752 feet**

Directions

Three miles
Allow one and a half hours

▷ There is a good car park in All Stretton. From here, walk along the B road that runs through the village and leads down to the main A49. The path you need is on the opposite side of the road. Climb the stile and head over the fields, keeping the lakes to your right. This path then winds through a small wood and just as it emerges into the open, take the path heading upwards on your right.

▷ After about 200 feet, the main path to the summit is there on your right. But it is a strange route up, so I would recommend heading for the ridge immediately in front of you, passing Three Fingers Rock. The summit of Caer Caradoc is about half a mile or so beyond that.

▷ For the return route, simply retrace your steps.

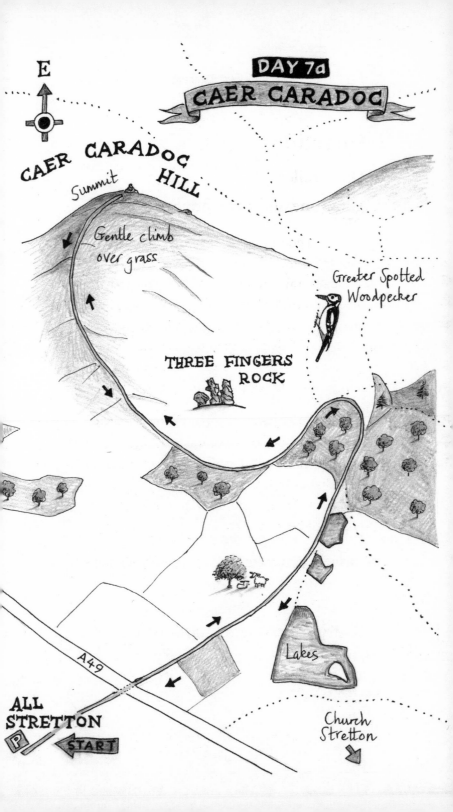

Pole Bank, Shropshire

Men are wearing shorts and car after car pulls in up to the banks of the stream flowing next to the road. Tables and chairs are being placed on even patches of ground and children are emerging from the back seats of cars wearing pink and orange sunsuits. An elderly couple are sitting on some garden chairs reading the papers; they both have straw hats. His long, heavy shorts are held up with a brown leather belt – not everyone comes to walk the hills.

Further up the road there is ice cream, coffee and a sturdy block of public toilets. It is 10 o'clock in the morning and there is a party going on. This must be the doing of the weather forecast and the promise of an open window of warmth. It's true there is not a cloud in the sky. It seems the army of walkers are of one mind: a mass escape. They are fleeing, hurrying out of the car park while holding on to the eroding reality that there is solace at the end of the valley. The only element that is missing is two or three women from a small town in America, all of whom are wearing headscarves, pointing up at the sky. Everyone is wearing a hat.

Once the metalled road comes to an end we scatter. I walk up a tiny sheep path that steers above the main route up onto the ridge. On a small bluff a young man is standing looking down on the steady line of walkers beneath him. He is wearing a rust-orange T-shirt and carrying a day-pack. We say good morning. What is this affinity, this not having to go through the motions? Perhaps we see the same view and what is held within it means as much to us both, but here the similarities end.

He is young and good-looking with deep-set blue eyes. His walking boots are expensive. Perhaps he moved up to Telford nine months ago to take a job with a company that had just relocated to a bigger building in a large business park just off the M54. He is doing well at work and most evenings is one of the last to leave. On Thursdays he plays five-a-side football with some of the lads from the print room and each morning he runs three or four miles. Recently his boss has started including him in some of the planning meetings.

The days are easier now, especially if he works late, but the evenings and weekends can still be hard. For the first three months he barely slept; two or three hours a night, that was all. The pain of not having her next to him; her scent, her breathing. He learned that sorrow is physical, that absence has colours and a climate all of its own. Still speaking in every cell was the prayer of being in her arms and the storm of her loss.

They hadn't spoken, not once, and shortly before he moved they arranged via email for her to pick up some things. And he dreaded the thought that she would say, 'I wish you well.' This handshake phrase, spoken in car parks at the end of meetings, a sterile seed, as easy as 'Have a nice day.'

She breezed round the house, almost laughing, they didn't speak. She said one or two of the things were not hers, that was all. When what belonged to her was in the car, she came and sat down. It was then he noticed her hair was different, slightly redder. She breathed in – she had the most beautiful lips he had ever known, the lips

of an angel – and they said it, 'I wish you well.'
Now he heard it, the sounding gong.

Soon after arriving in Telford he picked up a
walking magazine in the hairdressers. He bought
a day-pack, some waterproofs and a pair of boots.
Now, every weekend he walks into the hills, up
onto the summits. They are teaching him to see
beyond exile, to understand it as a place in himself
that he has always known.

It is true, as a child he would climb up to the top
of trees, find a fork in the branches and sit there
swaying, sometimes for hours. He is beginning to
sense that he is on a journey. Several years from
now he will wake up one morning and realise
that since she left he has in fact been descending,
finding his way down. This will only happen when
he realises he is on solid ground again. 'Take the
valley on the left,' he said.

Lightspout Hollow is a sanctuary. An unhurried stream is easing into pools. Delicate, small trees leaning over the water bear twisted roots, hard as heather, gripping the rocks and the crowds gone walking up the Jack Mytton Way. It is not quite peat, not that coal-black earth quite yet. This is richer moorland, there is honey already here and, in this valley, starlings and frogs. The path ends on the Shropshire Way. In the car park an elderly couple have placed a red and cream thermos in the middle of a small table. She is sitting on one chair, he is grappling with the other one. Walking through there is the vague scent of suntan lotion in the air.

Pole Bank is heaving; there must be at least 15 bicycles lying on the ground and enough lycra to make a parachute. The Duke of Edinburgh boys have formed a corral out of their packs and are sitting within it. In the grass are hundreds of millipedes an inch long and slate grey; each one has between 40 and 400 legs. When they are picked up they curl into a spiral and are utterly still. It is a strange form of defence – maybe it is to fool the slow-worms taking on a different form. Not quite as convincing as the bird-dropping beetle.

Halfway through their cheese and cress sandwiches, the Duke of Edinburgh boys are commenting on the plethora of millipedes. 'I cut one in half, burnt one and drowned one.' 'Why?' I ask loudly. They pretend not to hear. I ask again, 'Why?' They all look at me. I look at him. 'A big boy like you and a little creature like that. What did you do that for?' Others stop eating their sandwiches. 'Be kind.' The boy concerned looks crestfallen and hurt. And they fidget for a minute or two then start packing. Barely speaking they hurry off, they leave town.

It was not handled well, not well at all. Using anger to parry brutality, leaving him with shame. It was there in his face to carry for the rest of the day. It would have been much better to pick one millipede up, to let it rest in the palm, to have gone over and told him how beautiful it is, they are, what an extraordinary form the universe has given birth to, to have kissed it in front of them all. To have honoured the millipede, not to have dishonoured the boy. I am a fool.

At the top of Ashes Hollow the horses are feasting up to their flanks in grass and soon their coats will shine. There is one wide grey mare heavy with foal; it won't be long now. She will slip away, find somewhere alone to give birth, to drop the foal.

This is one of the most exquisite paths in England. There is contentment here, not just because there is blue sky above; the deepening valley holds warmth, the water plays. Maybe it is because so much is being born, leaves emerging, wings unfolding, eggs warm in a small silver bowl of horsehair and lichen.

There are no corvids, not a magpie or a carrion crow. It is as if the hunters haven't found this valley yet. We live on a carnivorous planet. Somewhere in the stars there are surely planets where life is complementary, where nothing is hunted. There is something pure here, something unbroken, that is awakening. Rain arrives, then sun – moisture and warmth bursting through; the seeds bearing leaves and petals and, in this nursery, milk.

A wren is singing loudly just before the unplanned climb up onto Yearlet. There is no path and no footprints, just a few ewes guarding their lambs. The sunshine is pushing the last of winter northwards mile by mile. It must be nearly 30 degrees but the water in the small stream running between Ashlet and Yearlet is chilled.

The earth has not warmed up yet and smells of yolk and cattle. Very few people must come up onto Yearlet; the birds have it to themselves, far from the enchantment of Ashes Hollow. On the summit is a small cairn surrounded by long green grass.

The car park has become a festival. A multitude of children have taken the banks of the stream. Two boys in Spider-Man sunsuits are in the water, moving rocks, constructing a dam, watched by a small girl standing on the bank in a peach-coloured tutu. There is smoke and music, the smell of sausages in the air. In one car are two young couples; on the back seat a young woman stretches her feet out of the window, her head is resting in her boyfriend's lap. She is laughing uncontrollably. All four of them are wearing mirrored sunglasses.

Near where the car is parked another small posse of children is running for ice cream, barefoot up the road. It wasn't so long ago the beach cafe in Cornwall was closed with sand at the door, and a young man in a worn sweater had cold hands as he cleaned a petrol pump with a sponge under a grey sky.

Perhaps right now he is taking a break, leaning against the wall at the back of the shop with his eyes closed, his face in the sun remembering the boy who had spent all afternoon digging the biggest sandcastle on the beach with one red spade. And how when he was standing on top of it he could see his mother walking between all the yellow and green striped canvas windbreaks coming towards him carrying an ice cream.

︿ 15,506 feet

DAY 7b POLE BANK

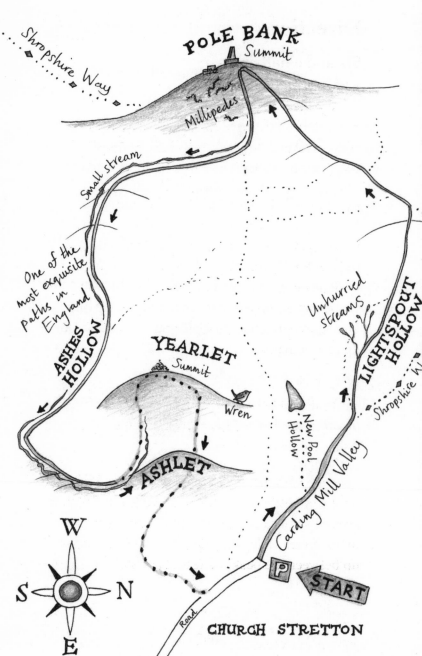

Shropshire Way

POLE BANK
Summit

Millipedes

Small stream

One of the most exquisite paths in England

ASHES HOLLOW

Unhurried streams

LIGHTSPOUT HOLLOW

Shropshire W.

YEARLET
Summit

Wren

New Pool Hollow

ASHLET

Carding Mill Valley

W N
S E

P START

Road

CHURCH STRETTON

Directions

Six and a half miles
Allow three hours

▷ You will need to arrive early in the day, especially at the weekend, to secure a parking place in Carding Mill Valley.

▷ From here, head north, passing the cafe and the toilets. There are only really two paths that head off to your left on the way up. The first will take you to New Pool: avoid this one. It is the next one you want, leading up Lightspout Hollow. This will take you to the Shropshire Way at the top of the ridge. Here, turn left, cross the road and follow the track up to Pole Bank.

▷ From Pole Bank, retrace your steps for about 150 yards and take the path on your right. This leads down to another section of road and the top of Ashes Hollow.

▷ Take the path that leads down into Ashes Hollow on the opposite side of the road. Follow the path for around a mile and a quarter until you see the last main stream valley on your left. This valley leads up between the peaks of Yearlet and Ashlet. There is a small rough path but it is predominantly rough walking up onto Yearlet and then down and back up onto Ashlet.

▷ From Ashlet, follow the ridge northeast for about 400 yards until you meet a good path and here turn right. This path leads back down into Church Stretton.

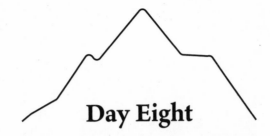

Day Eight

Kinder Scout, Peak District, Derbyshire

Music: 'Evensong (Sacred Night)'
by Nigel Shaw

Next to the metal bench that faces a yellow flowering tree is a cream and brown stoneware flagon. Around the base of the tree are three small standing stones rising up from a bed of grey gravel, which covers the entire garden. Next to the wall on the right is one small clipped green-leaved tree and right next to the tree is another metal bench. The sky is the same colour as the gravel.

It is a small garden, a yard really, at the back of this terraced house in Buxton. Small gardens are

often much more intense, more exact. They are intimate spaces because every leaf, every bud, is intimately known.

At the back of a house in Cambridge nothing is growing. It is enclosed in white walls on three sides. On the ground is a reef of different coloured glass pebbles with some larger lumps of yellow and red glass placed among them. In the centre stands a white electrically operated fountain and in the water are blue, green and aquamarine glass pieces. The fountain is lit at night.

In Brighton there is a small yard of ferns, some of them watered into the walls, others erupting from large flowerpots, and at night the lights have been placed underneath them; this is sanctuary.

In London Mrs Jefferson only grows pink flowers: carnations, sweet William, geraniums. The only relief from the pink is one white table with one white chair, where she sits and smokes.

There is a brief flash of sunshine in Edale and for a moment it becomes a hill village in Greece, with one narrow street and tightly packed small houses, to the west of which mountains of heavy grey clouds are rising. It is early and there are still a couple of parking places in front of the school. In the river, in the wood, the water is black, and after a sturdy bridge the path curves in stone across a field. Still the sun bears down.

The moor begins on the other side of a thin bridge, barely wide enough for a cat. The valley narrows and slowly the vegetation dwindles as the path turns to grit. It's there in every step, softer than gravel and louder than sand. At the head of the valley is Grindsbrook Clough, the entrance between the hill and the mountain. It's a steep incline of great grey angular boulders, almost half a mile of them. There is no symmetry here, there are no leaves. This is the work of ice and water digging their way downwards. Within a minute a mist sinks in and within five the boulders have darkened. What came before and what lies beyond is sealed; only dead birds fly in this confinement.

At the top of Grindsbrook Clough is a plateau and here the wind bumps the heather but the mist remains unmoved. Every so often thick drops of rain fall from nowhere.

Mikey is walking along looking at the screen on his mobile phone, which he is holding at arm's length in front of him. He appears out of the mist, leading a handful of bedraggled followers. He must be in his early 20s and looks as if he has just been for a swim. His hair, face, clothes and trainers are drenched. 'We are trying to find Kinder Scout,' he says.

One of the girls stands hunched and shivering behind him as if she was six and had been in the water too long. 'No, Mikey, *you* are trying to find Kinder Scout.' She is wearing a blue T-shirt and a thin waterproof, it's more a pac-a-mac (the ones that fold down into the size of an egg cup), and her pink underpants are leaching through her white nylon shorts.

The others are too fed up or too cold to speak. 'Follow the ridge west and then head into the plateau.' 'Where is west?' he asks. I lift my arm in the direction they have just emerged from. 'But maybe you should go down now, you all look very cold.' 'We are not cold, we are fucking freezing,' the young woman says. They slope away into the mist and just after they disappear completely the silence is broken by 'Mikey, you wanker.'

A middle-aged couple are also lost, as are two young men and a group of women in their 60s, all appearing out of the mist and asking where they are. We sit on wet black heather and take the maps out but they have been rendered unreadable.

Now that we are captives and blind beyond 30 yards, the contour lines and thin grey scrawls of rock and scree are indecipherable. The pro's would have taken a bearing and counted their footsteps, trusted in logic. But then they would not have dreamt there was a small gap in the rock just wide enough to squeeze through and long enough to lie down inside and watch the white air breathing before falling into a deep sleep.

Perhaps this is the gift of the mist, a becalming, the quietening. What happened before maps? Surely they would have waited until they could see again, waited in silence so as not to be found...? It is shelter of a kind. The sun for singing, the rain for drinking, the snow for warmth, the mist for reckoning.

Dan is wearing all the right kit: sleek grey waterproofs, a perfectly proportioned pack, and he is not lost. He is striding at speed and speaks faster than he is walking. He sets off, leading us over the heather and then through the middle of a granite outcrop.

All the time he is explaining that Kinder Scout is not the summit, it is no more than a tourist destination, that the true summit is barely visited and only known to a handful of souls. On the other side of the granite there are mounds and dips of black earth in some places that leave you sodden up to the knees. If it wasn't for the colour of our clothes, this would be a truly black and white land. Then Dan is gone, slipping through a group of walkers in front of us. At 10 yards we turn into vague shapes, we lose our definition, our outlines; at 20 yards we melt away.

It is strange that just one large boulder, covered in carved graffiti, seems to have been singled out by Pat, Harry, Seamus, Aman. There is no chalk here and the names underneath theirs have been rendered illegible by the rain and wind. The new names have been added over the old ones – it is an ever-changing tombstone, a rant against impermanence, up here where the earth meets the sky. Graffiti is taken from the book of loneliness, from alienation, it is where the revolution is written.

There are red grouse here. At least two of them are gliding through the mist. They favour wild land, they are the colour of foxes and autumn and will not fly down to the fields.

Kinder Scout is desolate and wet. There is only one woman here and she is holding a clipboard and completely covered in waterproofs, only her eyes visible, peering out of a balaclava looking for a group of runners to make sure they are all accounted for.

The summit is a small white-painted concrete trig point. It is the bare minimum, the only quarter given to human presence. There are no signposts – this is intentional, to give the mist its due and what is wilderness some oxygen. Up here on the plateau it is relatively flat and there are very few cairns. Now, in the mist, the bearings of the distance and the valleys are lost and we have all become wanderers and fast friends.

And when on the path leading down towards Jacob's Ladder the mist clears and we can see each other completely we let go of the names, of the hand we held in the hurricane, and become strangers again.

It is strangely dry at the bottom of Jacob's Ladder. A group of men are standing on a bridge over a thick stream at the base of the valley, looking up into the ceiling of mist above them. 'What's it like up there?' one of them asks.

'It's a different country.' The words just fell out.

Usually the fog comes in or the fret born on the sea slides onto the shore then inland. There isn't a choice about whether or not to enter it, and given the choice there is a real hesitancy, a natural resistance to walking up one and a half thousand feet into a world that has no more than a 30-yard radius. It is the other extreme; hills and mountains do not merely offer a panorama

but also the very real possibility of enclosure or being marooned or being lost. The mountain also gives the mist, and within it there is doubt, uncertainty, and the fear of never knowing home again. What shows itself in this place is what is real.

The birds have started singing again, announcing a change in the air, and the light on the fields here in the valley is brightening. Just before the farm that sits about a mile from Edale, an elderly woman is running her hand, her fingers, over a section of a drystone wall. When she turns and sees me she stops, and standing back from the wall she just looks at it. She is not dressed for hill walking, she is carrying an umbrella. She is petite, her skin masked in foundation, hiding all those years and what is hidden here.

Each stone is placed by hand; no machine is capable of laying stones in this way. In this section there are greens, magentas, blues and purples lying within the grey; it is exquisitely made. The wall is perhaps relatively new, maybe 60 or 70 years old, no more. Did he make it? He was good with his hands.

They would leave their letters here, tucked between the stones, arranging where and when to meet. Everyone walked to the dances then, from Malcote, Barber Booth, Castleton, Bradwell, from Goosehill. Sometimes it was a four- or five-hour walk over the moor to a dusty hall or a stone-built barn, swept in the afternoon. They would carry their best shoes in a shoulder bag, none of them had cars. And when it ended and you were thick with beer you would sing your way home, waking the dogs as you went, saving your last cigarette.

They were courting and her mother would say to her, 'Are there any flowers left in the fields then? He must have had them all by now,' meaning she was firmly of the opinion that the time had come for her daughter to have more to show for all this courting than violets, buttercups and cottongrass.

And it didn't take that long – just a couple of months – and there was another man who very quickly reassured her mother, who had learned that in love it is best to know what you want. That there were practical outcomes to be weighed: a ring, a roof, a table. That houses cannot be built with violets, buttercups and cottongrass. Over time her daughter learned that every room is cold without them and to love that which suits your purpose is to dig a dry well.

It is a hard last mile over the fields and then back down into Edale, following the brook through the trees. A small group of Americans have gathered outside the campsite cafe, just above the phone box, and we sit on a bench under a tree. A woman from Illinois asks how the shell ended up around my neck.

None of us noticed this big slice of blue arriving from the west over Jacob's Ladder, and suddenly there is sunlight changing the colour of the windows and the hills and immediately we stop talking and discover we are all overdressed in our waterproofs.

We stand up, looking at the sky. 'Well, this is a surprise,' she says.

It would have been good to be on the hill now. There would have been a minute, maybe two, when the mist would have been lit from above, when everything would have shone, turned golden as the veil was lifted.

ᐱ **17,557 feet**

Directions

Eight and a half miles
Allow four hours

▷ There is very limited parking in Edale so it is best
to park in the visitor centre and make your way
up through the village to the Old Nag's Head pub.
Continue walking past the pub, taking the track that
leads to Grindsbrook Booth.

▷ About 300 yards after the pub, follow the sign on
your right to 'Grinds Brook': the path leads down
over the brook and up the other side following
some stones laid across a field. These eventually
give out on the other side of a very narrow bridge.
Now, simply follow the path running alongside
the brook. At the head of the valley the path heads
right up a steep and rocky way. This tops out on
the plain.

▷ From here it is very hard going, especially if the
mist is down. Kinder Scout is not actually on a
footpath. The simplest route, once you top out
onto the plain, is to take the path in front of you;
this path leads directly to Kinder Downfall. Do not
get to the top of Grindsbrook and head left; this

will take you onto Grindslow Knoll. Staying on the main path to Kinder Downfall is also not easy; it is heavily eroded and the peat is very deep in places.

▷ Stay on the path for roughly a mile or so and you will notice various smaller paths on your right, which will take you up to Kinder Scout.

▷ From the summit, head back to the main path and here the minor path continues downwards towards the Pennine Way and Jacob's Ladder.

▷ Once you are on the Pennine Way, follow it down Jacob's Ladder, over Packhorse Bridge and onto Upper Booth. From here it is a straight run through the fields back into Edale.

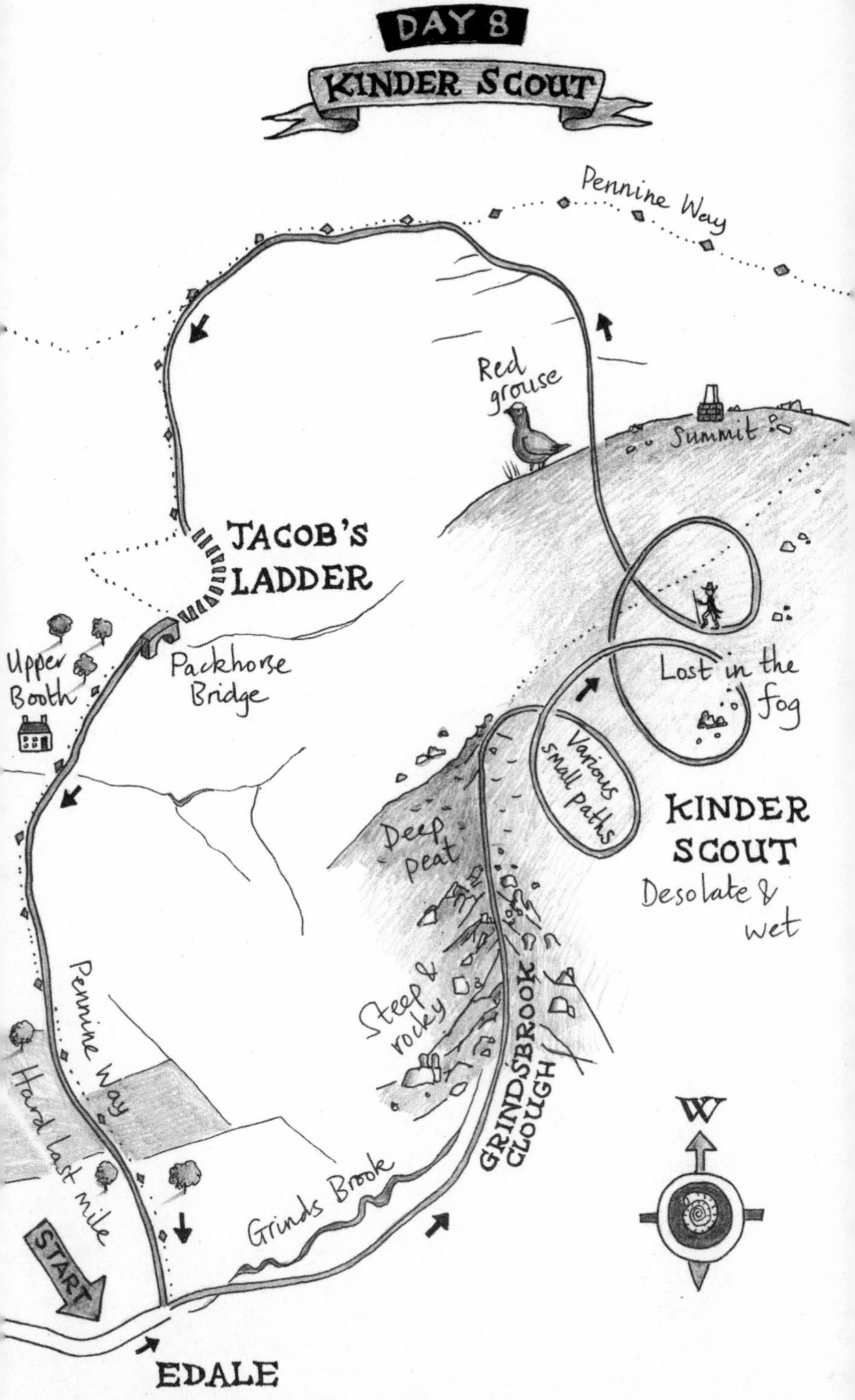

DAY 8
KINDER SCOUT

Pennine Way

Red grouse

Summit

JACOB'S LADDER

Lost in the fog

Upper Booth

Packhorse Bridge

Various small paths

Deep peat

KINDER SCOUT
Desolate & wet

Steep & rocky

Pennine Way

GRINDSBROOK CLOUGH

Hard last mile

Grinds Brook

W

START

EDALE

Day Nine

Haworth to Hebden Bridge, West Yorkshire

Music: 'Weird Fishes' by Radiohead

Hebden Bridge is around 100 feet beneath the base camp of Everest. At sea level the air contains 21 per cent oxygen. At just 1,000 feet this percentage begins to decrease. At 18,000 feet there is half the level of oxygen available and sense begins to fray.

Base camp is as far as most people go. Beyond base camp you are in ever-increasing danger and, because you are now much more vulnerable, fear kicks in. Fear announces itself in the need for reassurance, to constantly reaffirm you are not crazy to be here, tied to another human being, bound to each other. You place yourself in each other's care, in each other's fears, in each other's mercy, hauling each other higher now, into the heavens. From now on you barely eat, you barely sleep, and in the heavens, in the land of the gods, there is always delirium to contend with. It is not so much Marmite, raksi, boots and crampons that are put into the fire, it is you.

Hebden Bridge is water and stone, tight streets, the shops are small. The evening meal is rice and vegetables and only water. Lunch is normally more substantial: a couple of thick sandwiches, maybe a little smoked fish, some hummus, cheese and cress, some fruit. There are not many of us here and apart from one young couple and their newborn baby, sweetly sleeping on a sheepskin liner placed in a buggy, the rest of us are eating alone. There is almost an echo.

The waiting staff seem utterly disconnected, providing actorly smiles when required, but otherwise giving a bare minimum. There is no music. The elderly woman sitting at the next table stands up to go and glances at tomorrow's map on the table next to the glass of water, the route up Ease Gill and Great Coum folded inside. We exchange smiles. 'Have you been to the parsonage in Haworth?' 'No, I haven't.'

Her grey hair shines and her eyes behind her slate-rimmed glasses are blue and clear; she takes care of her skin. She looks at the map again. 'What's happening there?' I ask. 'It was the home of the Brontë sisters. You didn't know that?' 'No, I didn't.' ' Well, it's just over the hill, and I can see you have come all this way...' She pushes her chair back under the table and leaves.

There are five of us on the bus to Haworth, including the bus driver. He seems angry that he can't change gear so he keeps his foot hard down on the accelerator at all times and sighs audibly when he has to pull over to let the facing traffic through. There is a young man with dyed black hair and deep white skin, his clothing is black,

as are his shoes, the only concession to colour being one red stud in the middle of one ear that is almost dripping silver. He is plugged into music and doesn't move his eyes.

Both of the elderly women are wearing headscarves. They are sitting next to each other and they both have one hand firmly planted on the seat in front of them. The reason for this becomes increasingly clear as the bus leaves the outskirts of Hebden Bridge and pushes up onto the moor. The accelerator pedal is pinned firmly to the floor regardless of camber and corner. Now the two elderly women in headscarves start to lean in unison into each bend and, still talking, readjust their position to prepare for the next one.

On the way down the other side of the moor the grazing sheep on the side of the road are running for their lives. We tear through the outlying streets of Oxenhope and thankfully come to an abrupt halt in the centre of the village. Here, a blind elderly man feels his way to a seat followed by a troupe of sixth-form students who talk loudly as they file en masse to the back. Once the accelerator pedal is on the floor again, they make skidding noises to accompany each and every bend down into Haworth.

On either side of the cobbled street leading up to the top of the town are restaurants and shops selling candles, cashmere scarves and teddy bears. It is a grey northern day made all the more beautiful by a gusting wind. Everyone has their coats done up and their hands in their pockets but it doesn't feel as if it will rain – the wind is almost warm. It is a day for drinking soup out of a cup.

The young woman in the bookshop has long dark hair and green eyes. She doesn't wear make-up and seems completely at ease; there is a gentleness about her. This is a place of pilgrimage and every day she will meet people from all over the world for whom the ink is not quite dry.

The front door of the parsonage is at the top of some even steps and behind them is a neat, rectangular garden enclosed by a low wall. Beyond the wall dark gravestones lie still under moving trees.

What are we all here for, traipsing round these rooms? Emily didn't have her own bedroom, she shared a bed with either Charlotte or Anne and their bonnets are here, hanging behind glass. There are sentries standing next to the doorways; how many times have they explained there was no bathroom, that mealtimes were set, the table laid? This house is a shrine, not to the dead but to the wounded.

Now most of the men have taken their hats off and barely a word is spoken. The sentries stand quiet. Here you see what we can be guilty of: love, of loving, of not loving, of the lies that were laid and easily spoken, of the home betrayed just for one more touch of the skin on your face. Of confessing now to whoever they are: to him, to her, to the one we let go, to the rope we cut.

The path from the parsonage leads under the trees. They are just coming into leaf and being thrown around by a grey wind. A lost brown chicken runs ahead on the verge, nervous and looking out for dogs.

Emily must have walked this way and turned up the cart track running between two walls to the place where the trees give out to the moor.

It is a half-land at first, an uneasy coexistence, the fields and heather fighting it out over earth and sky. The sheep are unsure whether to stand or lie and there are bare patches of ground where nothing grows. At the edge of the reservoir, three lapwings are in the air. One circles and cries – there is a nest nearby. There is more bare earth on the other side of the wall that encircles the reservoir; enough for a scrape where the female bird can sit and be mistaken for dark and brittle heather. Where her chicks, when they hatch, can kneel and turn to stones. It is a much smaller body of water than Meldon Reservoir but still melancholic, something misplaced. It feels shunned. There is no one else around.

The bridleway that leads over the top of the moor is probably the old road from Haworth to Hebden. Who would want to ride or walk across the top of the moor in the winter storms? This is the route the crows will fly. What is now the metalled road came later, something easier for a coach and horses, kinder on the wheels, with far fewer small, steep sections. There are very few sheep here – this land cannot sustain them – and barely any trees: a willow or two in the hollows and occasionally a tattered stubborn elder. Here everything that grows is in debt to the rain.

The grey stone farmhouse on the other side of the brow is abandoned, it sits right next to the track. Once it was beautifully made, the stone window frames carved by hand. And inside there are shelves of stone and what is left of the range, the metal rotting, one door half hanging – there isn't a wire to be seen.

The ground is littered with the ceiling and half of the roof, a thicket of wooden joists half attached to what would have been upstairs and slates lying where they fell. At some point they must have packed up and left, probably between the wars, the children and the furniture all on a couple of carts creaking off the moor heading for Halifax, to some rented rooms or a terraced house.

Here, for a generation, they would be birds in cages. It's what Cathy became, run aground in the big house down on the plain, dying from the moment she arrived, a child waiting in her womb. Begging Nelly to open the window so she could taste one more gulp of the wild air, the storm blowing down off the moor.

On past the farm, the track straightens and is sinking into a valley alongside a thick running wall and to the east are more abandoned farms. One of them is large with evenly spaced windows. Surely Emily met them – Cathy and Heathcliff – as she walked over the moor, returning books and carrying letters into Hebden. She would have known the boy and the girl; seen them young and dirty, with eggs in their pockets, and passed them as teenagers in her Sunday best on an early summer's evening. They hardly saw her; she was barely there. They had their arms around each other; both arms. And she blushed. They didn't. They were not kept in by fences, up here on the moor, no one is looking, no one is whispering, you are judged by rain and dogs.

She blushed because for several seconds she found herself released from the wires of formal courtship, of the necessity of making a good marriage. How that need became everybody else's business and just how little her hips and her skin

and the fact that she did not know how to lie in a barn had to do with any of it.

Her breathing quickened and shallowed and once she was round the corner and believed she was out of sight, she sat down at the side of the track. Staring at the ground, the terrible understanding began to break through that any potential suitors, that those who were suitable, had been locked in the same room that she was in, that it was little more than a laundry, a place where all scent and sweat were removed.

Standing up, she began to brush the grass and bracken from her petticoats, removing all traces of earth; it was habit. That night, as half the moon rose over the moor, she sat by the window in her pressed nightclothes knowing they were lying unwashed and naked together in a single bed, a dog curled on the floorboards in the corner. Then she thought of dressing and going to the tavern but she did not have the compass to find it.

The wall runs almost to the bottom of a valley. The land is greener here and a wide brook has dug its way down and washed all the peat off the stones. The wind is quiet; it's a good place to sit and eat. On the other side of the valley a boy comes tearing down the road on a quad bike through the muted colours. When the engine is switched off, a dog starts to bark.

The sky is thickening, the air dampening. Now the track rises, cutting across the side of a steep slope. Further on is another abandoned house on its own and a vague path through tufts of grass down to a hard-locked door. Looking in through a broken window, the plaster lies on the floor where it fell and there are holes in the ceiling, wires leaning off walls, scatterings of dulled feathers, but the roof is good. There are the remnants of sunshine here, it is not forlorn – some laughter remains and some ease. Once there was kissing and the loving of children.

Beyond the house the hill rises and, from the brow, distant roofs and the dark hilt of Stoodley Pike thrust into the earth on a summit to the south of Hebden. Ewes and lambs are in the fields close to the farm and from here a stile leads into the trees. At the bottom of the slippery path is Hebden Water, young with rain. It is a long valley down under the trees following the water on a path laid with tree roots; there is nothing to be gained from hurrying, even if it should rain.

All the tables are empty at Gibson Mill, a lichen-coloured oblong selling blankets and coffee; the water guarded in the millpond with a curving bank is too dark to reveal any fish. It is now a wedding venue. Once there must have been sacks and horses, smoke from the chimney stoked by the diaspora from the moor. Now it's too harsh and too wet, with only a couple of months when the butter really softens and miles from any school...

All these reasons are emptying the moor, the wild land, leaving the wading light, the sound of rain on the yard, to give up the storm for something easier. To leave the high land for the mill, to choose the valley for what is apparently ordered, a more controlled environment, a straight street, tins of food. This will always ferment an exile because once we have laid in the storm, shared a breath of that air, taken in the scent, it is then within us, calling for our return.

The road above New Bridge, a mile or so beyond the mill, curves past terraces of neat houses. There are hyacinths and forsythia here, a mower in every garage. And at the junction, signposts pointing the way, and further on towards the centre of Hebden, shops, pubs, banks, a tourist information centre.

The small group of young goths hanging out on the bench next to the canal are looking for a way out of this order. Maybe they already know you have to be lost to find it.

⌃ **18,699 feet**

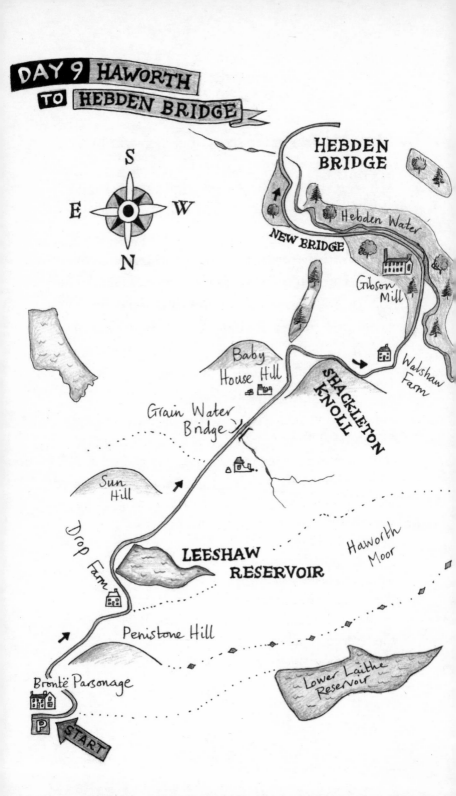

Directions

Six miles
Allow three hours

▷ The path out of Hebden Bridge runs along the bottom of the graveyard which stands in front of Brontë Parsonage. Follow this path out beyond the buildings and under the trees. After about half a mile there is a bridleway on your right, running between two low walls. Take this path, which leads upwards and onto the moor, out onto Penistone Hill Country Park.

▷ Take the footpath leading diagonally across Penistone Hill and follow it as it heads diagonally southwest over the moor. It comes to an end very near a minor crossroads. At the crossroads turn right, heading towards Drop Farm. The footpath you need is on your left and is signposted just beyond the farm.

▷ This path takes you down to the main wall of the Leeshaw Reservoir and from here joins the bridleway leading out over the moor and passing the reservoir wall on your right. This is a good path over the moor, passing abandoned buildings and reaching Grain Water Bridge after about one and three-quarter miles.

▷ From Grain Water Bridge, the path slopes diagonally upwards onto Baby House Hill Lane and to another abandoned house. Here, take the path that leads diagonally over the field and rejoins the main path having wound around the base of Shackleton Knoll.

▷ From here the path leads to Walshaw Farm. There is a stile in the corner of the field beneath the farm and the path on the other side leads down to Hebden Water. It is important to cross the river at Gibson Mill.

▷ It is a good mile and a half walk, following the river down through the wood to New Bridge, where you take the minor road that leads back into Hebden Bridge.

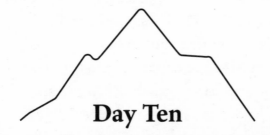

Day Ten

Hebden Bridge to Stoodley Pike, West Yorkshire

Music: 'Sunrise Of The Planetary Dream Collector' by Terry Riley

It is 6.30 in the morning. I need height. The wandering into Haworth and the lilt over the moor means this will need to be a big day.

In the upstairs windows of the converted mill buildings the curtains are drawn. An elderly man is walking his Jack Russell towards the bridge. They both move slowly. He is an early riser; sometimes he is at the newsagents before it opens and he waits on the other side of the road. He doesn't sleep much since Bessie died and the dog needs feeding. Their son works in Bahrain, they speak once a week on the phone.

The town is not awake yet and the pigeons have the square near the canal all to themselves. The sun is straining through a few openings of blue but it is losing confidence.

It is a straight run to Stoodley Pike but finding a way out of Hebden is confusing, it isn't at all obvious.

The field on the other side of the canal is heavy with dew and in the wood above it the rooks are fighting among themselves for the scraps of a fallen kingdom. They lose it every year as the shadows begin to shorten. This happens when the leaves arrive and spring takes hold – they are confined to the trees and banned from gathering in public until the end of September. They are sullen throughout the summer.

Foxes have made the path through the trees that sneaks to a break in the wall. On the other side is a pure green field and one jaunting magpie. The fields and the farms here are small. The stone walls laid down over hundreds of years have held, and on the way over towards Stoodley Pike, a thoroughfare turns between two high walls wide enough for flocks and herds. It is not used any more, not in the manner that it was built for. It is now an empty river – there is hardly any mud.

When the walls come to an end, the path runs straight over a field passing a small copse planted with silver birch; a separate enclave almost entirely surrounded by a curving wall. What was here before this oasis of white bark, moss and clumps of pale tufted grass? Spring has not yet arrived here, the temperature is lower; there is less light. This is the land of mice and shrews, the home of the lost sheep, a place of forgetting. There are these places set apart. They hold what cannot be contained within the walls of home. Here, what is unfolded cannot be seen – human beings come to these places so they may talk to themselves, so they may cry. Before the rise up to Stoodley Pike there is a farm and set further into the hill another abandoned house. Here the moor is taking back the fields.

Stoodley Pike was cast in Mordor: the sky wants it gone. Lightning hits it every so often; it is a dark sword in the ground, an emblem of war, a house of shadows – the birds seem to shun it completely. It is best seen in the mist.

On the way back down to Hebden the sun breaks through, sparkling the dew on the fields. At the edge of the wood stand a doe and her fawn, quiet, unhurried, here almost up to the hem of the town. Ewes and lambs are made of spring but they are here because the ram was put out for the tup, and she gave birth inside the barn with a slice of the best hay. She is not here of her own volition, whereas the deer can eat what she chooses and go where she pleases – she is a wild cousin. At night, walking between the walls then along the edge of the field and into the white-barked copse where the moon is cracked within the trees, this is where she lies down.

The town is waking up: children in blazers, people at bus stops, a lorry unloading outside the chemist. In a dream last night there was a mire, and beyond that a lane lined with fruit trees all in blossom, with children playing in the gardens that ran alongside them.

⋀ 19,664 feet

Directions

Four miles
Allow two hours

▷ Finding the way out of Hebden Bridge is not easy;
there are no signposts to lead you to the path.
So you can either start by heading up behind the
Co-op, where there are paths which will lead you
towards the telecoms mast at the top of the hill, or
you can take the minor road next to the Chapel,
which is towards the end of the high street and just
under the ridge. The path is on your left, leading
towards the mast. Either way, just before reaching
the mast, take the straight path heading south
towards Stoodley Pike, which is visible on the
horizon.

▷ This straight path is Pinnacle Lane, and once you
come to the end, turn left and follow the path. This
is a brief section of the Pennine Way, which leads
all the way round to Stoodley Pike.

▷ To return to Hebden Bridge simply retrace
your steps.

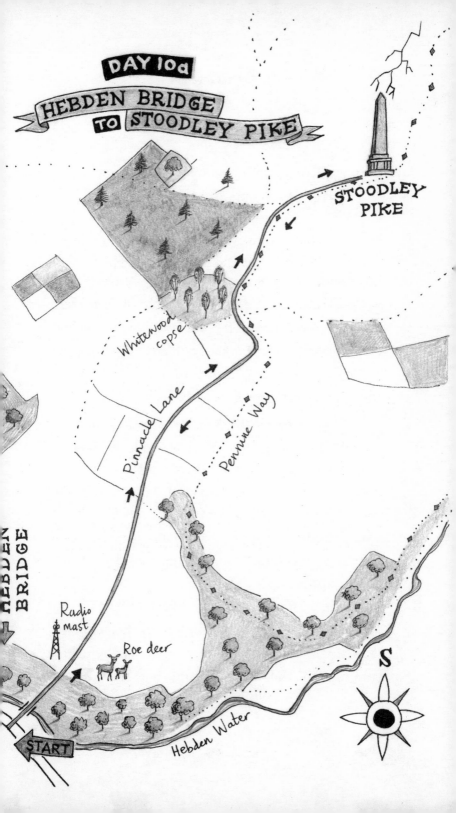

DAY 10a

HEBDEN BRIDGE TO STOODLEY PIKE

STOODLEY PIKE

Whitewood copse

Pinnacle Lane

Pennine Way

HEBDEN BRIDGE

Radio mast

Roe deer

Hebden Water

START

S

The Calf via Cautley Spout, Cumbria

This is a big hill. The top is cast in cloud and there is steady rain underneath it. No one else is in the car park and there are very few cars on the road. This is a lone walk. The presence and absence of other people always makes a difference.

On the very high mountains and in some of the deserts the presence of life – of birds, plants and animals – diminishes almost completely. Where there are no other forms of life you are truly alone and in these places just a glimpse of a bird can bring such reassurance, such joy. The rain is falling hard and the wood on the bridge over the river is slippery. The land darkens in the rain, the soil darkens, the trees darken, so does rock and heather.

In the distance are little spots of reds and yellows. There, almost at the top of the waterfall, is a small band of walkers. And in the valley running to the base of the hill, the horses stand motionless and the dips in the grass are becoming sodden. The grey wagtails, however, are dancing.

The way up begins in a fairytale, a stone staircase climbing the side of the waterfall, which is being pushed and pulled around by the wind. There is surely a wind speed beyond which we cannot hear ourselves think. This is a cleansing. Just 10 minutes is enough and you return with water pouring down your face and sit there recovering, coming round from a time of not knowing a release from the grip of the patterns that had hardened, enforcing normality, demanding all the energy of fascination.

At the top of the staircase the path flattens and turns to grit, edging to the point where the water becomes the waterfall. It is a boundary between two worlds. From the road at least, what lies beyond the top of the waterfall is out of sight. It is a small valley carved by the water and now enclosed and quiet with mist. It has done nothing to ease the rain which is falling evenly, lulling the earth as a mother calms her baby. Then voices and a queue appears. The issue is a large grey rock and around the edges a mire made of this year's boots. This is a group of around 10 people, some in yellow, some in red waterproofs, men and women, walking over the top then down into Sedbergh.

In the mist their faces are intensely beautiful. They must be in their 70s, maybe early 80s, but they appear to be ageless, their features moving between the child and the adult. They are helping each other around and up onto the rock, and one elderly woman who has managed to get above it just sits quietly in the mist and rain, looking out from under the hood of her waterproof. She seems to be completely at peace.

'Another mile or so,' they say. The path sinks deeper into the earth until it is about a yard beneath the rest of the land. It is simply a matter of stretching out your hand to reach the heather and the mist is thickening.

The summit is another white-painted trig point and there is no need for a view, not now. Much better just to sit and be alone, not to know what lies beyond, to let all the choices rest. The mist is a confessor.

It is hard to know whether they are really here, this line of elderly walkers intent on the summit. They are not speaking to each other although they walk at the same pace and are evenly spaced. Once they pass, they very quickly lose their definition. Just above the waterfall the mist clears; it hasn't moved an inch. Even so, it is hard right now to imagine stars.

⌃ **21,682 feet**

Directions

Five and three-quarter miles
Allow three hours

▷ There is a small car park near the Cross Keys Temperance Inn or you can drive a little further to a larger car park past Handley's Bridge.

▷ From the Cross Keys, take the footbridge leading over the River Rawthey and once across turn left. Follow this path down to the valley floor and here head up to your right, following the valley towards Cautley Spout waterfall. At the base of the waterfall the steps head steeply up onto the ridge. From here, follow the path around to the left.

▷ To reach the summit of the Calf, follow the path that runs southwest alongside Force Gill Beck. This path is sunken and rutted and runs for about two-thirds of a mile, eventually reaching the main summit path. Turn right and climb the short section up to the summit.

▷ To find your way back, simply retrace your steps.

AY 106 THE CALF VIA CAUTLEY SPOUT

THE CALF

Summit

Sunken & rutted path

Force Gill Beck

Red Gill Beck

Dales High Way

Sedbergh

Cautley Crag

CAUTLEY SPOUT

Waterfall

Stone staircase

Grey wagtails dancing

Cautley Holme Beck

Cross Keys

P

Footbridge

START

River Rawthey

W

S · N

E

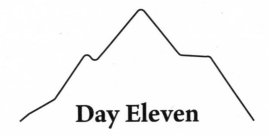

Day Eleven

The Cheviot, Northumberland

*Music: 'Turiya And Ramakrishna'
by Alice Coltrane*

There is water in this light: the sun comes straight off the sea. It was worth waking early for. Lindisfarne is still sleeping – a little square village on a low-lying island cut off twice a day by the tides. This island is a morning land, there is only this purity of light when the sun rises over the sea, or over the desert, when there is nothing in between and even a mile or so inland the intensity is lessened.

In that first hour it is as if the sunlight penetrates stone and wood and skin. The birds seem very tame here; this is a pilgrim island where people come to read and to listen.

There are very few clouds in the sky but the wind is still young – it has an unbroken colt in it. The valley leading to Langleeford is becoming more and more yellow; on some of the gorse bushes there is barely any visible green at all, there is this great bubbling of yellow out of the earth mixed with the gold of last year's bracken.

The road in is broken in places; half tar, half stones following the river in and it will not take any cars further than the farm. It is still early: the farm dogs haven't started barking yet.

The wind is just on the cusp – any stronger and it would be a battle and any lighter and it would be breeze. It doesn't feel like a farm track; there is nothing to farm that requires something this wide. It must be for the grouse, which are everywhere, tractors pulling covered carts filled with men and guns. The beaters sit out in the open in the back of Land Rovers, they don't tend to talk much.

The summit is hidden and there are no signs and several different paths all as wide as each other. The wind blows the map, nothing is still here. Every blade of grass is moving. And there is this light almost straight off the sea – the Cheviot is not that far from Lindisfarne; there is surely some salt in the air. Once the farm is out of sight there are no other houses, it is just the hills. The only sign of human activity is lines of fences. Posts and lengths of wire.

Scald Hill is a crossroads of sorts. Fences, a meeting of paths and only slightly more than a mound. Around it the land is rutted and the black peat bare. From here in places the path must be 50 feet wide and a couple of stolen fenceposts laid down offer the only way over the worst of the mire.

He smiles for 50 yards before he reaches me. Slung under his backpack is a tent and a mat. He is on his way down and is the happiest man on earth. He walks with a staff, not a stick, the wind throwing his long hair around his eyes. His features are more Norse than British but his accent and the lilt of his words come from nearby. As we shake

hands he just looks at me, into me. He breathes in, 'It's a fine day.'

Is this a Green Man? Who knows, there may be one or two left sleeping up on the summits, speaking with the stars, eating fish and tubers, drinking moving water.

'Where are you headed?' I ask.

'I am going this way for now.' He looks towards Scald Hill. He walks away from me and then shouts, 'Pilgrim!' I turn round.

He asks, 'Have you found it yet?'

'No.' He laughs and opens his arms, turns and faces the wind. 'Here it is, it is right here.' He smiles and then sets off again.

There is snow up on Comb Fell edge lying in a lee, safe from the sun. These hills must be white in winter. It is a steep rise up to the stepladder strung over a fence – on the other side is almost a wasteland. Large bare patches of black earth, tufts of grass now and again, occasionally a pool and running through all of this is a pavement without a road, curving over the summit plateau. Slabs of stone laid end to end, in the midst of all the natural forms cast and thrown by the wind and rain. The square stones lead to the square summit. What have we done? It is a place to come and cry.

Grouse butt number seven offers a little respite from the wind. I stop for an early lunch in the small circular enclosure. The sunlight is steady on one part of the inner wall.

There was no sign of the Green Man up on the top; no trace. It is not a place to sleep up there, not if you are travelling all the time. Far better to find a curved bank by the stream, somewhere with water and shelter. And to wait.

Maybe he was waiting for the sun to rise, to bring the bracken gold, to read the shapes of clouds moving across the side of Comb Fell edge. Maybe next week he will reach the sea, having spent three days and nights on the bank of a pond in the middle of a wood, waiting and watching for fish rising from the depths to the plain sight of the surface, sometimes breaking the film between these two worlds.

He had vowed not to return to the tenement in Barrow, not to go back until he could not remember the sight of his own face in the mirror that morning. He was so out of it most of the time he didn't see the mould and the rats by the bins. That was over four years ago now and in that time he has spoken with rivers and leaves, lost every complaint. It was a small box his life was in and it wasn't betrayal or callousness born out of fear, even though those things happened and they hurt. It was beauty. It wasn't what lay within the darkness that was overwhelming him, it was what lies within the light.

There is no sign of him on the way back to the car and no one else is parked up. Time seems to be fraying, all urgency has gone.

⌒ **23,775 feet**

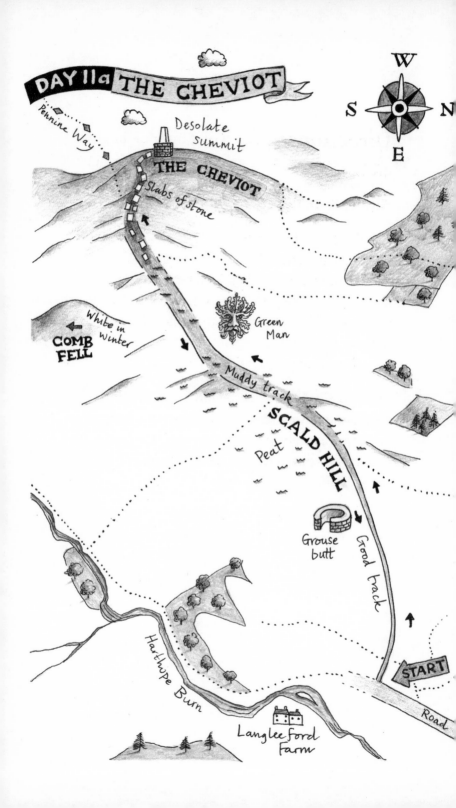

Directions

Six miles

Allow three hours

▷ The drive in following Harthope Burn and heading towards Langleeford can be bumpy but there is good parking at the end of the road near the white metal bridge. The path you need is the one heading west up the side of the slope towards Scald Hill. Do not take the path heading north as this will add a considerable amount of time to this ascent.

▷ Once on Scald Hill take the very obvious path heading southwest up onto the Cheviot. This path is extremely peaty in places. The last one-third of a mile or so is paved with stones that lead directly to the summit.

Dungeon Ghyll
to Pavey Ark, Cumbria

The New Dungeon Ghyll Hotel is all benches and tables, day-packs and sticks. This is a walkers' pub – pints of soft drinks and big bags of crisps: fluids and salt. It is mid-afternoon and there is still some sun on the flat fields running up the valley to the base of Langdale Pikes.

Jackdaws and sparrows are bartering in the car park and on the verge next to a newly cleaned black car, a young girl is crying. She must be four or maybe five. Her father is sitting on the grass in front of her and she is saying, 'I want Mummy, I want Mummy.' She says it over and over again in the midst of deep sobbing; genuine distress. And he seems almost defeated; maybe he is an inch away from opening the door of the car, lifting her into her seat and heading for her mother's house, which perhaps is not where he lives any more. He is also close to tears. He had collected her as arranged at 9.45am. This was a big day;

their first time together after all the absence, the papers, the courts and the bargaining. It had reached this point.

An elderly couple walk past, both of them using two poles. The woman stops and hands her partner her poles, takes off her day-pack and unzips it. While she is doing this, she is talking directly to the little girl. 'Well, I am looking at all these tears and all this sadness and do you know, I am hearing this sorrow deep in my heart.' Now she is crouching down in front of her. 'My name is Sandra and this is my special warm blue blanket.' It is actually a travel towel, the lightweight kind that folds up into little more than a tennis ball. But in her voice she has invoked a mixture of calm, fascination and trust.

And with barely a movement the blanket is around the little girl and the elderly woman takes the girl's hand and places it in the hand of her father, who has said nothing. She looks at him and says, 'Keep it.' She then kisses her fingers and places them briefly on the little girl's brown hair; she is now curled and quiet in her father's arms. This healing takes no more than 40 seconds.

It is a well-walked route up to Stickle Tarn. The stones are scuffed and the grit compressed. It is steep and the ghyll churns to the rain. Up ahead, a man's voice is calling 'Jasper!' The name bounces off the rock faces around the tarn. Again, 'Jasper!' ... then silence.

It is not easy to tell which dog is Jasper, if any of them. The collie doesn't seem to be a Jasper and she is followed by a Bedlington cross who is wet and appears to be sulking.

This is a popular hill and the morning walkers are beginning to descend. It is still bright and dry, lovely when the wind is light and the surface of Stickle Tarn is varnished and holding time still. This surface, on which everything is told, everything known and heard: they say it is a lovers' reckoning.

And before this path was here, the young man and the young woman climbed up to the lake where, if the water was still enough, they would see each other's true selves there on the silver spoken surface. In that reflection there was, there is, no separation, and here they could make one promise that would be impossible to

Day Eleven

break, given into the care of something deeper than flesh.

They lay on the bank, there between the worlds, and looking at her reflection he spoke these words, 'Breath of my breath, soul of my soul, love of my love, forever, forever.' But when the woman looked into the lake she could not see him, all she saw was her own reflection. So she said nothing and the wind blew over the water and a terrible silence fell between them.

Wherever he went from that day it seemed he took the rain with him, and she moved from mirror to mirror until one morning she woke and heard him speaking in the rain.

The afternoon sun has become a glowing orb in a grey woollen sky; maybe there are more autumn days up here than anything else. Winter is still alive in Jack's Rake, an outlaw in the wet rock, begrudging the dresses of spring, clinging to the scent of a cellar. My hands are cold.

Jack's Rake is a diagonal crevice running up the side of the sheer rock face under Pavey Ark, and there are places to fall from up here, especially near the top, with its wet and sometimes slippery camber that ends at the edge. It is a rite of passage, that step. That step, where if you slip you fall and when you fall you die. In dreams this can happen so quickly, this reality emerging from the midst of safety. A benign grass bank that suddenly turns precipitous and there are no handholds, no footholds and the falling begins and the terror wakes you. This dream is telling you that it is now urgent that you attend to just how much you are holding and that, physically, your body is in imminent and immediate danger if you continue on your current course. This is useful information that wakes you into the unflinching reality of where you are right now.

There are some small drifts of snow resting in between the rocks but it isn't necessarily cold. There is a point in these mountains when the late afternoon sun is almost horizontal to some of the rock faces. Way above base camp on Everest the sun sets beneath you. In seven weeks or so the sun will be at its highest point in the sky but warm nights here are rare. The orange glow on the rocks is cold to touch and the pink evening water in Stickle Tarn is colder still.

It is almost dusk on the Wrynose Pass, an old drove road, and over the brow to Cockley Beck and across to the dark surface of Wastwater. This road is a sweetness hung with spring and the gorse clamouring on either side. Wastwater is the deepest lake in England: the bottom 50 feet are below sea level.

The hotel bar is crammed with stories and underwater faces; platoons of men all eating big plates of food, back from patrol, from placing flags on peaks. Way beyond this room, Mars awaits and the moons of Saturn whisper. We hear but we do not understand, cannot understand, as long as we assume they are more alien than we are.

Right now the only option is retreat from all this noise: knives and forks, glasses and plates, the chords of bravado. There is nothing circular in the residents' lounge, there is no one else in here and the need for sleep is now overwhelming every cell. It is such a sweet feeling, the body craving rest. But there is something more gentle than that calling me. It is there, waiting on the summit of every hill, every mountain. I cannot name it. It is strange I do not feel alone.

⌒ 25,783 feet

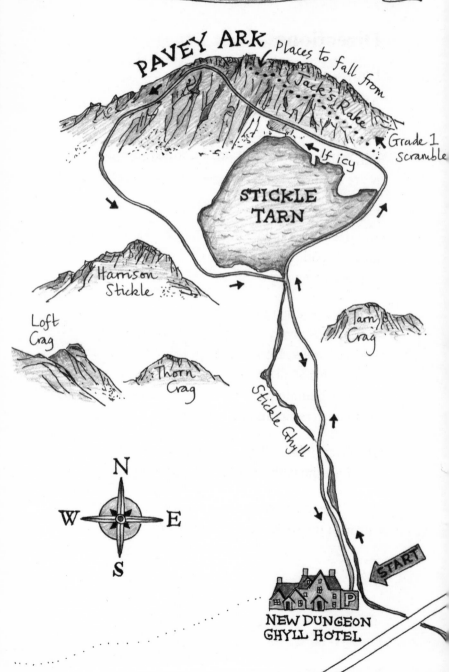

DAY 116 DUNGEON GHYLL TO PAVEY ARK

PAVEY ARK

Places to fall from

Jack's Rake

Grade 1 scramble

If icy

STICKLE TARN

Harrison Stickle

Tarn Crag

Loft Crag

Thorn Crag

Stickle Ghyll

N
W E
S

START

NEW DUNGEON GHYLL HOTEL

Directions

Four and a half miles
Allow two and a half hours

▷ There is very good parking at the New Dungeon Ghyll Hotel. From here there is only one main route up to Stickle Tarn, which simply follows the beck upwards.

▷ At Stickle Tarn follow the lake around to the right and this path will take you to a small section of zigzags leading upwards to the base of Jack's Rake.

▷ Jack's Rake is a grade one scramble and getting to the top will involve using hands and arms as well as feet and knees. Do not attempt the ascent up Jack's Rake if it is at all icy – it can be dangerous and you will definitely need the right clothing and kit, including crampons and ropes.

▷ If it is icy, follow Stickle Tarn around to your left and take the path leading upwards onto Pavey Ark.

▷ From the top of Jack's Rake simply follow the cairns through the rocks up onto the summit.

▷ I would not advise coming back down Jack's Rake, so from Pavey Ark summit take the ridge path heading initially down towards Langdale Pikes, then pick up the very obvious path leading off it down to Stickle Tarn on your left. From here, follow the lake round and then retrace your steps back down alongside the beck to the car park.

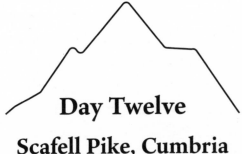

Day Twelve

Scafell Pike, Cumbria

Music: 'Call To The Wind'
by Carrie Tree

The cloud base is down, waiting halfway up on every slope, grey and impossible to bargain with. This has to be one of the deepest valleys in England, enclosed on three sides.

They say the Vikings came here, that some of the roof timbers in the church are from a longboat. What is certain is that the limits of the agricultural revolution are visible, drawn in straight lines of stone onto the hills. The maze of walls arranged into fields that lie beyond the Wasdale Head Inn, that sit so firm on the plateau, reach up the slopes

237

and at some point they simply go no further. And beyond that point it is only dogs that can herd sheep; the land is fresh off the press and the streams that come with the rain do not have names. It is just before eight in the morning and there is a dusk in the air, somewhere nearby there is rain.

No one has walked across this field yet. There are no footprints in the dew and the sweet charm of small birds – finches and sparrows – feeding from one hawthorn to another is joyful. The winter is done and the birds are ripe with courtship, they have been dancing for several weeks now, the male wrens singing. Even the crows are smiling. Nests are being made, weaves of hair and grass, scented moss, then the quiet of eggs; sitting and breathing, nothing more.

After the wooden bridge the path is eating into the earth up to Lingmell Gill, which is the colour of snow. On the other side of the water a stone stairway is rising steeply into the clouds, way past where the walls end.

A step at a time, then into the mist, and after a strange wide gritted track, there is an alleyway through the rocks lined with cairns and pools of snow. Stay on the path. Now the way is twisting through a land of stones. The mist thickens and the wind shouts louder. The path splits. Put a marker down, a coin, memorise the colours and forms of these stones.

The cairns are bigger now: silent sentries standing every 20 yards, each one invisible to the next. Then there is a small rise and it is here – the summit – and so are they. There are no words spoken. All these miles and these thousands of feet ascended, and now in this hurling noise, their silence.

Yes, what brought me here? No one lives in this empty house, in this temple without a roof, in this thin place. Wait here for the healing and drink. Drink this milk until you are quenched, speak, have your sorrow heard, open and your love will be known.

I leave the blue stone from under Brea Hill on top of the summit cairn. It is wet with tears. It feels as though the wind is coming from every direction, and there is snow here lying in pools. It is some way below freezing.

It is time to go down now. In six weeks' time there will be fields of buttercups and at sea level the water will be warm.

Five hundred feet beneath the summit four women are adding more layers, they seem serious, we barely speak. And further down, just under the cloud base, two young men are almost running up the steps. They have come from Ben Nevis and are doing the Three Peaks Challenge. They ask how much further it is to the top.

At the base of the steps, near where the path crosses Lingmell Gill, a very pale young man is struggling; he is nearly broken. He asks if I have seen his two friends and it is clear he feels abandoned by them now that he can't keep up, now that he really can't do it.

Mountains test relationships, they strip you down inch by inch until all that is left is the truth, and this usually emerges when things become difficult, when the plan breaks. This is when relationships are also broken.

In extremes there is never anyone to blame. Once we reach the point when personal survival kicks in, most of us become ruthless and that is when other people get hurt.

None of this was apparent all those weeks ago in the bar, sinking pints, drawing straws and agreeing to take it in turns to drive. Now he is on the verge of being beaten, his face grey and anxious with the thought, the knowledge, that if he turns back it will affect their friendship, maybe break it in time.

'Take it at your own pace, it's early in the morning, there's no rush, find the pace that you can manage.' He looks doubtful, he wants permission, to stop, to lie down. 'Find the pace that suits you, that's all you need to do right now.'

There was still some way to go – maybe an hour and a half, maybe less, and four hours, maybe five in the car down to Pen-y-Pas and the beginning of the route up the Miners' Track to the summit of Snowdon.

'Let's sit down for five minutes, drink some water.'

On the path just before the bridge, before the field, is one blue egg. And in the field it is almost summer, almost warm, and I can hear the flies and the water has calmed slightly, is easier, in less of a hurry, still dancing. The rain in service to the sea, the sea in service to the land and the earth in service to life.

I need about 20 feet more height and so I climb the fir tree in the corner of the churchyard.

I am a boy again now, walking out through the first field and into the second; the sky is an endless blue. One day a spaceship may sail its way through this blue towards another star and we may step onto another earth, but this time not to conquer, no, only to connect.

⌃ 29,004 feet

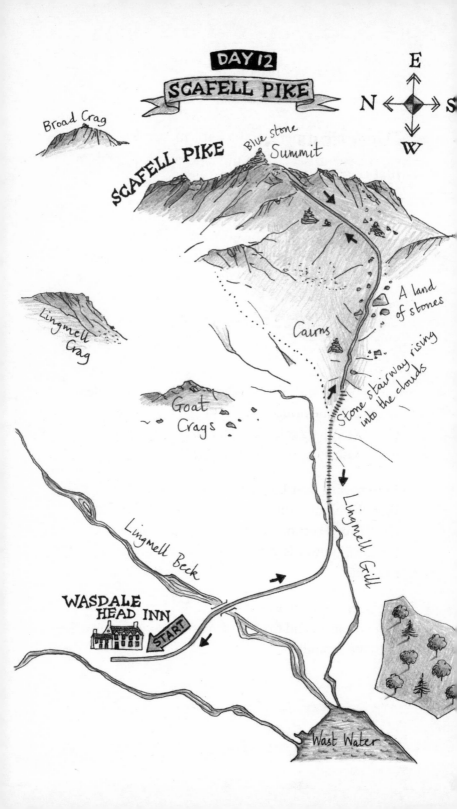

Directions

Just over two and a half miles
Allow three hours

▷ While this is described as the 'easiest' route up the mountain, it is still a long, hard yomping climb and should not be underestimated.

▷ From the Wasdale Head Inn, walk the minor road until you reach a gate on your left. This leads over a delightful field to the bridge which crosses Lingmell Beck.

▷ Cross over the bridge and follow the path up to your left. After a mile or so this joins up with the path coming up from Brackenclose.

▷ The crossing over Lingmell Beck is very obvious. From here, carry on up the paved path. This joins a good section of path at the top and follows the cairns upwards. Always remain on the main route up.

▷ In the final section the cairns become bigger and more frequent and following these will lead you up onto the summit.

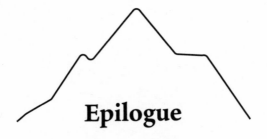

Epilogue

Music: 'Download'
by Mezzowave

A pilgrimage consciously sets out as an exercise in connection. You walk with the other. You carry the other and the other carries you. There is an outcome, a destination – you head for an altar, for a hill, a shrine, for a thin place. The terms are set; it is a discipline. This is the route, this is the way. The purpose is to arrive and the journey is framed by those who have walked it before, in the tradition in which it is held.

Pilgrimage is a common theme that links many religions and perhaps in the future they will acknowledge this as common ground, the

common living ground of the earth. The word 'pilgrimage' still retains its resonance, its promise, and taking this long walk as an act of devotion is now experiencing a mysterious renaissance. Is the sky devoted to the earth?

Some friends of mine periodically set off on a 'vision quest'. They do this alone and there isn't necessarily a route to follow, it is more of a process. Here, the purpose is to uncover what has been engulfed by routine, by conformity and, to a certain degree, to face what has been placed in the shadows. They are much heavier than we realise.

A vision quest reveals what we are carrying and why we have chosen to carry it. It is also a quest for revelation; for something to be revealed which would not otherwise have come to the surface. In the normal bustle of existence we would certainly have missed it.

Some people set off on a vision quest with a question, and what many of them say is that while the answer was not immediate, the vision quest cleared the ground and played a pivotal part in the process of arriving at it.

Most of us simply get used to the geography around us. The geography of rooms: where the pictures hang, where we put the chair. Most of the books stay where they are once they reach the shelves. The soundscape of the street, of the rain arriving from the west. These things very quickly become familiar; the lamp stays in its place and we forget it is marking time between the end of another day and the beginning of another night.

And life is told in the graves of dogs and Christmas cards, in weddings and the crocuses of spring. In the film 'It's A Wonderful Life', starring James Stewart and Donna Reed, the main character, George Bailey, played by James Stewart, is almost brought to his death by what he assumes to be an endless reel of work, food and sleep. It is an extraordinary film about the beauty of intimacy and how all of us act as catalysts for each other.

George Bailey spends most of the film wringing his hands at what he believes to be the 'ordinariness' of his own life. The film, which appears on television almost without fail every Christmas, cements the reality that we don't need to go anywhere else. It is classic agrarian propaganda, that life is happening in front of us if only we would wake up to it. It is a beautiful truth and, within the film, a beautiful sleight of hand.

George Bailey was rescued from his crisis by an angel. Maybe we are constantly rescued. The film really feeds the dogs of home, life on the plain, of sticking around to pay the mortgage, the bills and the monthly payments on the car and this is all just to keep us steady, checking in. The radio plays and we wake up and work and then go to bed again. Maybe we'll take a holiday, sit on a beach, and yet whatever unfolds, the mountains wait, they wait for us.

I remember seeing them for the first time. Before then, as a boy (I must have been about 12), I travelled to Switzerland, to the Alps. There was a slow train journey and the train eased through the mountains and beneath the tracks was a copper sulphate blue river and in the forests running alongside the ski slopes the squirrels were black. There is a memory of a street in Switzerland and some golden scissors cast in the shape of a stork but even in the midst of the mountains I did not see them. Even being within them I have not one view to remember them by.

The first time was in the Arans in Wales, barely more than hills. I remember being nervous – it is humbling, an essential lesson, the first lesson for the novice. Now I know I should have shaved my head, brought a garland, laid it down upon the summit in return for the gift of the view. Yes, this new view, it was just a sliver glimpsed from the back seat of a car. It seemed white and yellow and vast. We had been building up to it, starting on Dartmoor and then into the New Forest and on a three-day walk through Dorset. This was preparation for these nursery hills, low enough to walk the dog. But they led us into the mountains, into Snowdonia, the north face of Tryfan and the 90-mile-an-hour winds on Yr Elen.

And into the Lakes and up to Torridon, to the Cuillins rising out of the sea on the Isle of

Skye. Then over to Ireland, the Big Gun on the MacGillycuddy's Reeks. I used to be frightened, shaking almost, on Crib Goch. Not any more. I have been a pupil now for 20 years and they have taught me well, the lessons on fear, on insecurity, the reality of impermanence, the necessity of risk, the innocence of the leaves, the ceaseless poetry of water.

Really this journey should have begun in Wales, on Cadair Idris. Three nights alone on the summit and on the third night you stay awake until dawn. You come back down to the plain after that, either a madman or a poet. It is a rite of passage; a statement of intent.

The others have slipped away into families and work and the lattice of friends; we send each other Christmas cards and occasionally speak on the phone.

But for me, it is not a choice, I have to return. It is a calling; the mountains speak your name. Sit and look at them, give them some distance, you will know if you are being invited onto the summit. There is always a reason.

They are visible from miles around and, here on the map, these bumps and lifts are seen reaching upwards as the satellites stare down. They call us out of our straight, constructed streets and serve to free us from the cold, cold grid we have placed over the land. The blocks, the fences, the millions of miles of wire, boundaries, borders, oh yes – and alphabets, numbers and instructions – all of this policed by the gangsters on the plain, charging for this, charging for that. The wounds of avarice, the cuts of injustice, the lapwings dying in their thousands, numbed and dressed every morning at quarter to eight by 'Thought for the Day'.

Even so, most of the larger hills haven't yet been taken. Here in Sussex, the Downs reach up between Firle and the sea. There are one or two farms up towards the tops but for the most part the land is free from housing. Not many people in England live above 2,000 feet. And the further north you journey, the more untouched the higher land becomes.

The higher land is invaluable because it is primarily unfenced; there is not the order and the certainties of the plain on offer here. Above base camp you really can get lost and die, especially if you are left there alone. The storm will distil you down and you will have to decide what to hang onto. I will not call them desolate places – no, this is the work of the sirens of the plain, imposing roses and barley and barefoot meadows on our psyche. Above 2,000 feet we are seen by ravens, heard by silence. Here, we are not the orphans of the wild that we have become on the plain.

Coming home, coming back down; returning is often the hardest part, simply because the reckoning has changed us, whether it is the reckoning of death, the reckoning of fear, of the grey seas of absence, or, of course, the most brutal reckoning, which is the reckoning of love and of not being loved. The one vine, the sweetest wine.

We return to the same bed where she does not lie, we return to the same broken pieces, but they cannot cut us any more if we have now forgiven, if we return bringing gratitude.

There is no set time for resolution, but the hills, the mountains, offer the space and therefore the very real possibility of reaching it. How long you carry her for, how long you carry the knife they used, how long you see his face reflected in the water, churn the anger, is for as long as it takes to see beyond it. That is the pain of ascent, the gift of the summit. This is where we meet the dragons and the giants and the sage.

As I write, the clouds are very much darkening over the future. Much of what underpins the present was spoken in the wilderness. It is surely time we heard her song again.

Author's Acknowledgements

There is no reason the trig points on the tops of some of the hills and mountains in England should be notable. They are predominantly concrete, some are painted white, and perhaps the ones that sit most easily are those made from the nearby stones. But I must thank all who have made them: millions of people have placed their hands upon them. The work of the Ramblers' is also invaluable and all of us who walk the paths of this land are in their debt.

It would be extraordinary to take into account all who have made this journey possible: the hen that laid the egg, the hand that lifted it from the coop, the provider of the seeds for the cress, those who planted and grew the rice in the gluten-free bread, the rice in the restaurant in Hebden Bridge... The road gangs that laid the tar. The weavers of sheets, the makers of water bottles.

While this was a journey made on the island of Britain, it was facilitated by a global community; the global community of human, avian, mammalian and bacterial beings. Isolation is a dangerous and tragic illusion. We live in communion, in a state of interdependence that is the reality that underpins existence, and it is beautiful, and we have barely begun to explore it.

I must thank the poet Jay Ramsay for his ever-generous encouragement. Also I give thanks for the work of Martin Shaw and his ability to raise to the surface the living forms of archetypes there waiting for us at the edges of history and at the limits of therapeutic knowledge.

Thank you to all who gave me a bed for the night and to the growers of the food that was fuel for the journey as well as to the makers of maps and boots and socks.

Thank you, Donna, for your patience, for your light pen and your forbearance. Thank you, Sarah, for the maps. Thank you, David Peters, Andreas and Vicky Kornevall, Jen White and

Author's Acknowledgements

Lilian Simonsson for your wise counsel. Thank you, Hels, for your grace. Thank you, Vanessa and Jimmi, for Calypso, and The Ram Inn in Firle for the Rioja.

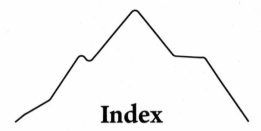

Index

Index

Index

Index

V

Velvet Bottom, Somerset 106
Victoria, Queen 127–9
Vikings 237
violets 174–5
vision quests 247–9

W

wagtails, grey 209
Wales 252, 253
walking poles 59–60
walls, stone 173–4, 203, 237–8
Walshaw Farm, Yorkshire 198
warblers 24, 110
Wasdale Head Inn, Cumbria
    237, 245
Wastwater, Cumbria 230
water, drinking 17
waterfalls 208–9, 212
waterproof clothing 17
weather forecasts 18, 32
weddings 37, 45–6
'Weird Fishes' (Radiohead) 181
West Highland terriers 97
West Midlands 125–40
West Okement river 69, 70
wheatears 82
whistles 17
white admiral butterflies 119
Whiteleaved Oak, Worcestershire
    136–7, 139
whitethroats 24, 110
'Why?' (Mezzowave) 87
wild men and women 30–2
willows 189
wolves 110
woodpeckers, greater spotted 142
woods, walking in 66

Wookey Hole, Somerset 102
Worcestershire 125–40
Worcestershire Beacon 127–9, 139
worms 126
wrens 156, 238
Wrynose Pass, Cumbria 230
Wuthering Heights (Emily Brontë)
    189–92

Y

Yearlet, Shropshire 156, 159–60
Yes Tor, Devon 64–7, 71–2
Yorkshire 181–213
Yr Elen, Snowdonia 252

Picture credits

AA Media wishes to thank the following photographers and organisations for their assistance in the preparation of this book.

16 Flowers and Gardens by Jan Smith Photography /Alamy Stock Photo; 26 mauritius images GmbH /Alamy Stock Photo; 38 Gabe Palmer /Alamy Stock Photo; 47 Mike Hill /Alamy Stock Photo; 54 Michael Newgass; 61 Tim Gainey /Alamy Stock Photo; 68 foto-zone /Alamy Stock Photo; 80 Peter Adams Photography Ltd /Alamy Stock Photo; 99 James Osmond /Alamy Stock Photo; 118 Tim Gainey /Alamy Stock Photo; 128 A ROOM WITH VIEWS /Alamy Stock Photo; 135 Michael Newgass; 144 tim gartside landscapes /Alamy Stock Photo; 152 Michael Newgass; 164 Michael Newgass; 172 Dennis Jönsson /Alamy Stock Photo; 184 Tetra Images, LLC /Alamy Stock Photo; 191 Glasshouse Images /Alamy Stock Photo; 199 Jake Eastham /Alamy Stock Photo; 218 Oliver Smart /Alamy Stock Photo; 227 YAY Media AS /Alamy Stock Photo; 240 Michael Newgass; 248 Sergey Parantaev /Alamy Stock Photo; 254 YAY Media AS /Alamy Stock Photo.